Praise for *Belonging to the Universe*

I found the book both interesting and exciting. The authors bring out with welcome clarity the important meaning that the new paradigms in science and theology have for the Earth and all of her creatures. Their dialogue goes beyond mere intellectual curiosity with the evolution in science and theology. With the excitement of seekers after a greater truth, they probe the processes of life and the spirit to find the striking interconnectedness of all reality. I recommend this book for both the beginner and the advanced in the fields of theology and science. The depth that the authors reach is accessible to all.

—Matthew Fox
Author of *Creation Spirituality*

Belonging
to the
Universe

Belonging to the Universe

**Explorations on the
Frontiers of Science
and Spirituality**

Fritjof Capra
David Steindl-Rast

with
Thomas Matus

HarperSanFrancisco
A Division of HarperCollins*Publishers*

FIRST EDITION
Text design by Victoria Vandeventer

Library of Congress Cataloging-in-Publication Data

Capra, Fritjof.
    Belonging to the universe : explorations on the frontiers of science and
spirituality / Fritjof Capra, David Steindl-Rast with Thomas Matus.—1st ed.
        p.   cm.
    ISBN 0-06-250187-9 (alk. paper)
    1. Religion and science—1946– 2. Philosophy and science.
I. Steindl-Rast, David. II. Matus, Thomas. III. Title.
BL240.2.C27 1991
291.1′75—dc20   90-56454
                                                                      CIP

91 92 93 94 95 RRD(H) 10 9 8 7 6 5 4 3 2 1

This edition is printed on acid-free paper that meets the American National Standards
Institute Z39.48 Standard.

Contents

Preface

"When winter comes to most other areas of the northern world, spring is already advancing in Big Sur. Here, springtime comes suddenly with the first hard rains of December or even of late November. 'Winter' in the Big Sur is really the advent of a glorious green and flowering spring." These words of the writer F. Schmoe apply also to Big Sur's climate of the mind. Here the California spring stirs at the root of a new thinking that may still lie dormant in frozen soil elsewhere.

New thinking is not necessarily superior for being new, but neither is it necessarily worse than the old. It deserves to be given a hearing. It needs a forum where it can be presented, discussed, evaluated. Big Sur has a forum of this kind: the Esalen Institute. For well over two decades now, ideas and methods first conceived at Esalen made an impact on other parts of the world later on. This pioneering of methods and ideas, this intellectual midwifery at Esalen brings to mind the names of Aldous Huxley, Abraham Maslow, Fritz Perls, Buckminster Fuller, Stanislav and Christina Grof, Alan Watts, Gregory Bateson, Charlotte Selver, Joseph Campbell, Michael and Dulcie Murphy—this list goes on and on; and so do the cultural ripples that started here, often with quite a splash.

The conversations recorded in this book also took place at Esalen. At a symposium on "Critical Questions About New Paradigm Thinking," held by the Elmwood Institute in late 1985, Fritjof handed out a list of characteristics for "new-paradigm thinking" in science. Somewhat tongue in cheek, David and Thomas produced a look-alike parallel for theology. Soon it became obvious that our witty little scheme had far-reaching implications. Exploring these implications for several years, we meet at Esalen once in a while to discuss the parallels, point by point. The present book was distilled out of these conversations. Its pages bear the imprint of Big Sur with its incomparable beauty.

This ought to be an illustrated book. Yet what illustrations could capture the changing light in the eucalyptus trees, the ever-changing coloration of sky and sea? What could convey the fragrance of that garden perched on cliffs above the sea, the sound of breakers thundering deep down below? The warm, heavy smell of compost, the wind's sound in the cypresses, the gurgling of the creek under the wooden footbridge were so intimately interwoven with the mood of our dialogues that readers might smell and feel and hear them unawares. Wine tasters, after all, taste the soil in which the grapes grew.

Although this setting in nature is not explicitly mentioned in our text, it was an essential element of our conversations. The sense of belonging, which lies at the heart of spiritual awareness, became the central theme of these intellectual encounters; and having them in such a magnificent natural setting—embedded in nature's cycles of light and darkness, of burning sun and soothing mist, of serene calmness and frightening thunderstorms—made us experience that sense of belonging more vividly than our most animated discussions. Our constant shared experience of a dialogue not only among ourselves but also with the Earth helped us again and again to reach intuitive understandings and tacit agreements where words had to be left behind.

We like to think that the Earth, our Great Mother, is present on every page of this book, and we hope that for readers who sense her presence the most obvious shortcoming of the book, the absence of a woman's voice in the dialogue, will be less painful. Gaia, the living Earth, is the silent source of everything we say in these conversations. She gives us the context for the new thinking about God and Nature.

Big Sur, California, August 1990   *Fritjof Capra*
                                                      David Steindl-Rast

Acknowledgments

We would like to express our gratitude to

— Steven Donovan, Nancy Kaye Lunney, and Michael Murphy for their generous hospitality at the Esalen Institute, where the dialogues recorded in this book took place;

—Vanja Palmers for his encouragement and financial support;

—Lorilott Clark, Nancy Graeff, Robert Hale, Joanna Macy, Raimundo Panikkar, John-David Robinson, and Margaret Van Kempen for reading parts or all of the manuscript and offering valuable comments;

— our editors John Loudon and Holly Elliott for their fine and sensitive editing of the text; Paula Hand for administrative help; and, last but not least, Wendy Ellen Ledger for her superb transcriptions of the audiotaped dialogues and careful word processing of countless drafts of the manuscript.

New-Paradigm Thinking in Science by Fritjof Capra	**New-Paradigm Thinking in Theology a paraphrase by Thomas Matus and David Steindl-Rast**
The old scientific paradigm may be called Cartesian, Newtonian, or Baconian, since its main characteristics were formulated by Descartes, Newton, and Bacon.	The old theological paradigm may be called rationalistic, manualistic, or Positive-Scholastic, since its main characteristics were formulated in theological manuals based on Scholastic proof texts.
The new paradigm may be called holistic, ecological, or systemic, but none of these adjectives characterizes it completely.	The new paradigm may be called holistic, ecumenical, or transcendental-Thomistic, but none of these adjectives characterizes it completely.
New-paradigm thinking in science includes the following five criteria — the first two refer to our view of nature, the other three to our epistemology.	New-paradigm thinking in theology includes the following five criteria — the first two refer to our view of divine revelation, the other three to our theological methodology.

1. Shift from the Part to the Whole	**1. Shift from God as Revealer of Truth to Reality as God's Self-Revelation**
In the old paradigm it was believed that in any complex system the dynamics of the whole could be understood from the properties of the parts.	In the old paradigm, it was believed that the sum total of dogmas (all basically of equal importance) added up to revealed truth.

In the new paradigm, the relationship between the parts and the whole is reversed. The properties of the parts can be understood only from the dynamics of the whole. Ultimately, there are no parts at all. What we call a part is merely a pattern in an inseparable web of relationships.

In the new paradigm the relationship between the parts and the whole is reversed. The meaning of individual dogmas can be understood only from the dynamics of revelations as a whole. Ultimately revelation as a process is of one piece. Individual dogmas focus on particular moments in God's self-manifestation in nature, history, and human experience.

2. Shift from Structure to Process

2. Shift from Revelation as Timeless Truth to Revelation as Historical Manifestation

In the old paradigm it was thought that there were fundamental structures, and then there were forces and mechanisms through which these interacted, thus giving rise to processes.

In the old paradigm it was thought that there was a static set of supernatural truths which God intended to reveal to us, but the historical process by which God revealed them was seen as contingent and therefore of little importance.

In the new paradigm every structure is seen as the manifestation of an underlying process. The entire web of relationships is intrinsically dynamic.

In the new paradigm the dynamic process of salvation history is itself the great truth of God's self-manifestation. Revelation as such is intrinsically dynamic.

3. Shift from Objective Science to "Epistemic Science"

In the old paradigm scientific descriptions were believed to be objective, i.e., independent of the human observer and the process of knowledge.

In the new paradigm it is believed that epistemology — the understanding of the process of knowledge — is to be included explicitly in the description of natural phenomena.

At this point there is no consensus about what the proper epistemology is, but there is an emerging consensus that epistemology will have to be an integral part of every scientific theory.

4. Shift from Building to Network as Metaphor of Knowledge

The metaphor of knowledge as building—fundamental laws, fundamental principles, basic building blocks, etc.—has been used in Western science and philosophy for thousands of years.

3. Shift from Theology as an Objective Science to Theology as a Process of Knowing

In the old paradigm theological statements were assumed to be objective, i.e., independent of the believing person and the process of knowledge.

The new paradigm holds that reflection on nonconceptual ways of knowing — intuitive, affective, mystical — has to be included explicitly in theological discourse.

At this point there is no consensus on the proportion in which conceptual and nonconceptual ways of knowing contribute to theological discourse, but there is an emerging consensus that nonconceptual ways of knowing are integral to theology.

4. Shift from Building to Network as Metaphor of Knowledge

The metaphor of knowledge as building—fundamental laws, fundamental principles, basic building blocks, etc.—has been used in theology for many centuries.

During paradigm shifts it was felt that the foundations of knowledge were crumbling.

In the new paradigm this metaphor is being replaced by that of the network. As we perceive reality as a network of relationships, our descriptions, too, form an interconnected network representing the observed phenomena.

In such a network there will be neither hierarchies nor foundations.

Shifting from the building to the network also implies abandoning the idea of physics as the ideal against which all other sciences are modeled and judged, and as the main source of metaphors for scientific descriptions.

5. Shift from Truth to Approximate Descriptions

The Cartesian paradigm was based on the belief that scientific knowledge could achieve absolute and final certainty.

In the new paradigm, it is recognized that all concepts, theories,

During paradigm shifts it was felt that the foundations of doctrine were crumbling.

In the new paradigm this metaphor is being replaced by that of the network. As we perceive reality as a network of relationships, our theological statements, too, form an interconnected network of different perspectives on transcendent reality.

In such a network each perspective may yield unique and valid insights into truth.

Shifting from the building to the network also implies abandoning the idea of a monolithic system of theology as binding for all believers and as the sole source for authentic doctrine.

5. Shift in Focus from Theological Statements to Divine Mysteries

The manualistic paradigm of theology suggested by its very form as "summa" or compendium that our theological knowledge was exhaustive.

The new paradigm, by greater emphasis on mystery,

and findings are limited and approximate.

acknowledges the limited and approximate character of every theological statement.

Science can never provide any complete and definitive under-standing of reality.

Theology can never provide a complete and definitive under-standing of divine mysteries.

Scientists do not deal with truth (in the sense of exact correspon-dence between the description and the described phenomena); they deal with limited and approximate descriptions of reality.

The theologian, like every believer, finds ultimate truth not in the theological statement but in the reality to which this state-ment gives a certain true, but limited expression.

Introduction

➤ **FRITJOF CAPRA (hereinafter Fritjof):** At the beginning, we would like to introduce ourselves and say what our motivation is for this dialogue. For my part, I grew up as a Catholic and then turned away from Catholicism for various reasons. I became very interested in Eastern religions and found very striking parallels between the theories of modern science, particularly physics (which is my field), and the basic ideas in Hinduism, Buddhism, and Taoism. This discovery also went hand in hand with a strong personal transformation. I had always been a spiritual person. I came from a spiritual family. And so I turned toward Eastern spirituality and over the years worked out a personal spiritual path that is actually influenced by all three traditions—Taoism, Buddhism, and Hinduism. It's influenced very strongly also by what we are calling now deep ecology.

Until recently my personal path did not really include Christianity at all, or at least not consciously, let's say. The change came just before my daughter was born. Brother David and I had a discussion, I remember. You told me that some time before, you had performed a baptism that was half-Catholic, half-Buddhist, for somebody.

➤ **DAVID STEINDL-RAST (hereinafter David):** It was actually *all* Catholic and *all* Buddhist.

FRITJOF: So I got very interested in that, and I thought it would be wonderful to have this for the baby my wife, Elizabeth, and I were expecting then, and that's actually what happened. David kindly arranged it, and we had a very beautiful ceremony. At that time I committed myself to give my daughter a spiritual education or to provide a spiritual environment that would *include* the Christian tradition. So, of course, my personal interest in Christianity was rekindled, because I felt I had to be serious about following through on that commitment. Now Juliette is two, and soon she'll be at the age of stories. I want to tell her tales from the Mahabharata and the other Indian stories, the Buddhist stories, and some of the Chinese stories. But I certainly also want to tell her Christian and Jewish and Western stories of our spiritual tradition and Sufi stories, too. Now, if I were to tell her the story of Christmas today, I could do it in a very simple way. But suppose she were five years older. I think I would get in trouble, you know. I wouldn't really know how to formulate it in a way that fits with my scientific and "Eastern" views of reality.

Another aspect of my concern to reappropriate my Western Christian tradition is that I lecture a lot in Germany, Switzerland, and Austria. And there the position of the Church is really very different from here in California. I don't think there has been a single lecture or seminar where somebody has not asked, "Where is God in your world system?" It just comes up all the time. The whole worldview is much more theistic than here in California, at least among the "New Age" or "new paradigm" crowd. And that seems the case in mainstream North America as well.

More recently the Churches in Germany—both the Catholic and the Protestant—have been very interested in the New Age movement and have been very scared by the new spirituality that is now emerging also in Europe. They feel they have to deal with that phenomenon (as mainstream Christianity does here also), and I am now invited all the time to these discussions. I spoke in Munich at the Catholic Academy of Bavaria, which had arranged a conference on "The New Age Movement and Christianity." And I spoke in Stuttgart to an organization of the Protestant Church with a similar theme. This is a discussion that is very lively now in Germany—the new spirituality and how it relates to Christianity.

It is these interests that bring me to this dialogue, and I really look forward to freshly discovering the meaning, the vision of Christianity, of the Judeo-Christian tradition, in our conversations.

DAVID: You mentioned that Buddhist-Christian baptism or initiation, Fritjof. It might be worthwhile to say a few words about it for a start.

The ceremony took place at Green Gulch, the Marin County farm of the San Francisco Zen Center. The parents were both ordained Buddhist priests, but they were also practicing Christians at the same time. You find this more and more in various Zen centers—that people who originally rejected their Christian faith and went into Zen, now maybe ten, fifteen, twenty years later, rediscovered their Christianity on a much deeper level through the Zen practice. Now they even want to have their children introduced into the Christian tradition. A child's baptism is simply the beginning of an initiation into the tradition. Since these two traditions are perfectly compatible when rightly understood, it was possible to introduce this child at the same time into both traditions. The whole sangha there and a very large group of nonmembers participated in the ceremony with deep appreciation and ready understanding.

FRITJOF: I think there's another point also. With a child it's not just because of a personal relationship with that faith that you want to introduce her to Christianity. It's also because Christianity is part of her environment. Just as it will be difficult but necessary to introduce her to death when an animal dies or when her grandfather dies, or to introduce her to violence or meanness, we will have to introduce her to these things, because they are part of the world. On the more positive side, the religions are part of the world, and she will grow up in a Christian environment. So even if I were not attracted to Christianity, I would have to be serious about introducing her to it.

DAVID: And the initiation is more of a promise than a realization, just an openness toward something that will come. We actually wrote in the little handout that we had for the ceremony: "Some Christians as well as some Buddhists who participate in this ceremony today may not feel very comfortable with it yet. But we should look at it as a promise. When this child has grown up, we will be much closer to the fulfillment of this promise. This child's generation will understand how compatible these two traditions are with one another."

That leads me to the second point you spoke about. Now you feel comfortable telling your daughter the stories. But when she's a little older, it may get more and more difficult. Many people find this to be so. The reason is that many of these stories had to be presented to us in a form suitable for children. But we were not encouraged to retell them at a later stage in a form suitable for adults. We need to rethink them.

There are adults who on every other level may be adults but with regard to their religious formation are really children. This may be especially true for scientists and other professionals even if they are practicing Christians, Jews. They can not speak about their religion in adult terms. You have a wonderful opportunity to grow with your child. When you are telling fairy tales, for instance, they have a different meaning for a child than for an adult. As adolescents we throw them out and think they're just nonsense. But as we mature we come back to them and appreciate their deep meaning.

As for my own background for these discussions, I also lecture often in German-speaking parts of Europe. I too am often asked, "How does the New Age fit in with the Christian faith?" And I am invited to conferences for scientists and representatives of religions, where we have to answer the same questions. Hence my great interest to know more about science.

I started out as an artist. That was my first love and interest in life. Then I got interested in primitive art and children's art. So I switched more and more over toward psychology and anthropology and finally got my doctorate in psychology. But at that time in Vienna we tried to make psychology an exact science, as scientific as possible. We were not the couch types of psychologists but decidedly the rat types. Everything had to be measured. That was my own interest, too. So I do have a taste for science and a great interest in a dialogue like this. I became a monk only after I had gone through training in art and psychology. The longer I am in the "professional pursuit of religion," if you want to call it that, the more I discover the great importance of art and of science for the fullness of human life. Hence the importance of the dialogue also for me personally. That's another parallel between us. It's not just because we have to talk publicly about science and theology that we are interested in their relationship, but it is a personal concern for both of us, Fritjof, for all three of us, in fact, I'm sure.

➤ **THOMAS MATUS (hereinafter Thomas):**   The complex relations among art, science, and religion are vital for me, David. However, my background is quite different from yours and from Fritjof's, because I was not raised a Catholic; in fact, I was not raised with any particular institutional religion. Both my parents—my father being of a Polish immigrant family, and my mother, the daughter of a Baptist minister—

had a very strong religious upbringing; but by the time I came along, they had withdrawn from the institutional forms of religion. For this reason, they encouraged my interest in spirituality, without imposing any particular religious practice on me.

As I was growing up, my mother was reading New Age literature and even a bit of Oriental philosophy. When in my early teens I also discovered Hinduism and Buddhism, they immediately rang true to me, although I'd also had some contact with Christianity, having read the Bible and attended Baptist Sunday school occasionally.

My first introduction to Oriental religions was through *The Autobiography of a Yogi* by Paramahansa Yogananda. In his book Yogananda quotes two British scientists, Arthur Eddington and James Jeans, with reference to the new scientific paradigm that was already emerging in the 1930s. This piqued my interest simultaneously in Yoga and in theoretical physics. I read some popular books on relativity and quantum mechanics, and although I understood very little of the math, I at least realized that the new physics was something that ought to be connected with spirituality.

In one other respect, my experience was different from that of David. Even though I was not brought up in a church, by the time I was sixteen I was convinced that my calling, my destiny was to be a monk. Whether I was to be a Hindu monk or a Christian monk was a question that I had to settle later.

I eventually joined the Camaldolese Monks here in Big Sur, and of course that entailed my embracing traditional Christianity. During my college years I had become convinced of the truth of the Catholic faith and was ready to accept the Church as my guru. But I still had some unanswered questions. Fortunately a Chinese Benedictine monk in a monastery near Los Angeles advised me not to reject what I'd learned from other religions. This was back in 1960, before the Second Vatican Council and the new openness in the Catholic Church. Meeting him at that moment in my life was a great blessing. He told me, "You wouldn't be where you are if you hadn't come through what you've come through, so you can't possibly discard it."

When I entered the monastery here in Big Sur, I encountered a certain amount of resistance to this ecumenical spirit; as a novice I was forbidden to study Yoga or Oriental religions. But I held on to the hope that eventually I would have the opportunity to do so. And as it happened, I did.

So in spite of our different backgrounds, we share many common interests.

Now let me say a word about how we started our dialogue. When the two of you were exchanging correspondence on Fritjof's criteria of new-paradigm thinking in science, David asked if I would help prepare a parallel schema of criteria for theology. All three of us were pleasantly surprised at how close some of the parallels were, and this led to the idea of recording our conversations on new-paradigm thinking. So now I'll be listening in and offering occasional observations from the history of theology and the history of religions.

Science and Theology

FRITJOF: To begin with, I'd like us to talk generally about the relationship between science and theology. The notion of a paradigm shift comes from science, and if we apply it to theology, we have to see whether that is justified. So I would like just to ask some very general questions. Basically, what is the purpose of science on the one hand and of theology on the other? What are their methods? Then I would like to say something about progress in science, and that will lead us to discussing the notion of a paradigm.

1 The Purposes of Science and Theology

FRITJOF: The purpose of science is, I believe, to gain knowledge about reality, about the world. Science is a particular way of gaining knowledge, next to many other ways. And one aspect of the new thinking in science is that science is not the only way, not necessarily the best way, but just one of many other ways.

The term *science,* to me, systematic knowledge of the physical universe, is recent, as you know. In the past it was called natural philosophy. So science and philosophy were not separated. In fact, Newton's first mathematical formulation of science in the modern sense is still called Mathematical Principles of Natural Philosophy.

Science and domination of nature

FRITJOF: Today the purpose of science is almost synonymous with domination and control over nature and is very closely linked to technology. There are many scientists, like myself for instance, who are not interested professionally in applications, but only in pure science, in gaining knowledge about the world. But even in that pure science, the idea of control has become very closely associated, almost synonymous, with the scientific method, and this is very unfortunate.

Many of us in the new-paradigm movement believe that this association of man dominating nature, which is a patriarchal attitude, has to be divorced from science. We would like to see emerge again a science in which scientists cooperate with nature and pursue knowledge in order to learn about natural phenomena and be able to "follow the natural order and flow in the current of the Tao," as the Chinese sages put it. That is how I understand the traditional medieval notion of pursuing science "for the glory of God."

This, then, brings me to the question, What is the purpose of theology? and How is theology related to religion on the one hand and to spirituality on the other?

Spirituality and religion

THOMAS: I can put it in the form of an axiom. You can have spirituality without religion, but you cannot have religion, authentic religion, without spirituality. You can have religion without theology, but you cannot have authentic theology without religion and spirituality. So the priority belongs, in my opinion, to spirituality as *experience,* a direct knowledge of absolute Spirit in the here and now, and as *praxis,* a knowledge that transforms the way I live out my life in this world.

FRITJOF: What is religion then? An institutionalization of that spirituality?

THOMAS: Institutionalization is one of the consequences when an original spiritual experience is transformed into a religion. But most important, religion brings out the intellectual dimension of spirituality, when it seeks to understand and express the original experience in words and concepts; and then it brings out the social dimension, when it makes the experience a principle of life and action for a community.

DAVID: I find it important to distinguish between "Religion," which we might write with a capital *R,* and "a religion." These are two quite different things. Raimundo Panikkar compares Religion with Language. Humans have Language, but nobody can speak Language; you have to speak *a* language. That's an important insight. You can't have Religion except in the form of *a* religion. You can't have just pure Religion, just as you can't speak pure Language.

Religion, as I use this term, should be written with a capital *R* to distinguish it from the various religions. Religion in the full sense of the religiousness from which all religions flow, as from their source. Translated into everyday living, Religion becomes spirituality; institutionalized, it becomes *a* religion. In itself it is the encounter with mystery, something we remember from our peak experiences. You could also say that our religious instinct as human beings is a thirst for meaning. In a peak experience we find meaning. For those moments, everything makes sense—life, death, everything. "This is it!" we want to cry out; this is what we have always been vaguely longing for. It's like an insight—not a clear idea or concept—an insight through which our restless search finds rest for a brief moment. It's a dynamic kind of rest, in no way static or complacent: a sense of belonging that urges us on with new longing. In this dynamism we see the core of Religion.

FRITJOF: Can you say a little bit more about this experience? Is that spirituality?

DAVID: Well, I use the term *spirituality* differently. Specifically used, spirituality would be the acting out of this experience, of Religion (with a capital *R*) in every aspect of daily life. Spirituality lets meaning flow into daily life. If you had this peak experience, and you shook yourself off and lived afterward as before, there's no spirituality.

FRITJOF: So spirituality is a way of being that flows from the religious experience.

DAVID: Yes. Spirituality lets Religion flow into your eating, into your writing, into clipping your fingernails.

FRITJOF: Let me ask you, then, about Religion, about this insight. At the everyday level, I can also have an experience "where I rest," when I gain an understanding of some technology or something or of everyday matters that would not be religion. What's characteristic of that particular "meaning within which we find rest"?

DAVID: Well, we all carry with us a great question. There is something questioning within us. It's an unexpressed question most of the time, or perhaps always. Our very life is a quest, a questioning. And once in a while, for no particular reason, we suddenly know the answer, we glimpse the answer. But the answer is not yet spelled out. We just say, "This is it." It may just be the smile of a baby in a crib. A parent looks at the baby, and there, "This is it." It is this kind of being able "to rest in it" from our restlessness with which we normally pursue life. Is this something that resonates with you?

FRITJOF: Yes, but what I want to get at is something else in spirituality or Religion that is very important for me. It is the sense of connectedness to the cosmos as a whole. That's also in the smile of the baby. The smile of that baby is my smile, because I am the father, but the smile of *any* baby is also my smile. And the smile of a dolphin—if you can call it a smile—is also my smile. That's what Gregory Bateson meant when he called it "the pattern which connects the orchid to the primrose and the dolphin to the whale and all four of them to me." So this sense of connectedness with the cosmos is essential to religious experience for me.

THOMAS: Could we use the expression *belonging?*

DAVID: Yes, that is the one expression I usually use—belonging.

THOMAS: *Belonging* has a double sense. When I say, "This belongs to me," I mean that I possess something. But when I say, "I belong," I don't mean that something possesses me, but that I take part in, am intimately involved with, a reality greater than myself, whether it's a love relationship, a community, a religion, or the whole universe. So "I belong" means "Here I find my place," "This is it," and, at the same time, "Here I am."

DAVID: "I am home." Maybe one can now use another image. I said we go around with this quest, with this question. Maybe one can say we often feel orphaned; we feel lost; we feel we're wandering and looking for something. Then comes a moment, unexplainably, "Now I am at home, this is my home. And I belong. I am not orphaned. I belong to . . ." This is often explicit, but sometimes just implicit. "I belong to all other humans." Even if there's nobody around, this is clearly felt. I belong to all the animals, to the plants. And belonging means I am at home with them, I am responsible for them and to them. You see, I belong to them as much as they belong to me. We all belong together in this great cosmic unity.

Then the great question is, How does one get from there to the religions that we see around us? Or even to one's private religion?

At least three steps are necessary here: theology, morals, and ritual. First, the intellect steps forth. That's where theology comes in. Here is our closest parallel with science. When we have an experience, and particularly one that deeply moves us and existentially involves us, we must think about it, reflect on it, come to know it better. And that's where I see the place of theology. Theology is the effort to understand what Religion implies. It is our intellectual playing with and working at the religious experience of belonging.

Theology

FRITJOF: Etymologically, the root of religion is connectedness. And the root of theology is in *theos,* God. But the way you present it, it does not require the concept of God.

DAVID: It does not require the *name* "God." And I am always very careful not to say "God" unless I know that the people with whom I speak feel comfortable with it, or at least don't misunderstand it too greatly. The term *God,* is so easily misunderstood that it is just as well to use it only with great caution.

THOMAS: Originally the term *theology* was applied not to the systematic study of religious dogmas but to the mystical experience. There's a famous saying by a Christian monastic writer who lived around the year 400, Evagrius Ponticus: "If you truly pray, you are a theologian, and if you are a true theologian, you will know how to pray." This, as an axiom, as a motto, gives the definition of theology as penetration into the unnameable mystery.

DAVID: May I come back to the sense of belonging and of being at home? If we use the term *God* correctly—correctly meaning in the sense in which the deepest, the holiest people in all the different world traditions would use it and would agree on its use—if you use it in that sense, we mean by God the reference point of our belonging. The one reality to which we ultimately belong and which therefore most intimately belongs to us can be called God.

FRITJOF: "Theology," then, would apply specifically to Christian theology?

DAVID: I think, you could use it wherever you have a theistic religion, a religion that speaks about the ultimate reality as "God."

FRITJOF: Anyway, in this dialogue we are using it in the Christian sense, I suppose.

DAVID: Yes, we are, but I would not like to limit it; one could bring in insights from other traditions that would qualify as genuine theological insights.

FRITJOF: Let's plan to do that in our conversation. Now, to come back to the nature of religion, you were talking about three steps, David, theology, morals, and ritual. So far, we've only been talking about theology.

Morals

DAVID: Yes, the other two do not concern us here so much, but when you have a religion, as opposed to Religion, you have not only theology or doctrine, which is the intellectual way of dealing with this experience. You also have morals, the dos and don'ts that spring from that sense of belonging. If you really have this strong interior experience of belonging, then implicitly you know that it calls for a certain way of living. Moral rightness consists in behaving as people behave when they belong together.

In this great Earth Household of ours, one has to behave like a member of this household; otherwise something is wrong. There are certain things one does in order to get along with the other members of the family. Therefore morals is immediately related to a cosmic reality. We have truncated it if we only speak about human behavior toward humans.

FRITJOF: So the second step is morals?

DAVID: Yes. Doctrine comes about when the intellect deals with religious experience. That's theology. But there is more to our religious response than our intellect. The sense of belonging that is so characteristic of our peak experiences gives us boundless joy. What gives us joy makes us desire more and more of it. "Yes," we say to ourselves, "my relationships to all others should spring from this sense of belonging. That would be paradise on earth." And so our will—our willingness—is activated to move toward what eventually becomes ethics or morals. What else is morality but our willingness to behave as one behaves toward those with whom one is united by a strong bond of belonging?

Ritual

DAVID: The third step involves our feelings. Not only the intellect and the will but also our feelings respond to the experience of ultimate belonging, and there's where you get ritual, the celebration of that experience. Ritual is meant to celebrate over and over the experience of our deepest belonging.

FRITJOF: So the feeling of gratitude, which is maybe one of the first arising in this belonging, would then be expressed in ritual.

DAVID: Yes, indeed. It is with gratitude that spirituality begins, with a sense of gratefulness for being alive, gratefulness for the gift of this universe to which we belong. In the give and take of daily living, every action can become a grateful celebration of this belonging. Ritual in this sense is an essential aspect of spirituality: a grateful celebration of life.

Science and theology

FRITJOF: So let's then concentrate on the first part, on the intellectual part. From what you say, science and theology are both reflections on experience. In science it would be the experience of the everyday world in a very systematic way. And, by the way, I want to talk mainly about natural science, not the social or human sciences.

So in the natural sciences we are concerned with natural phenomena, and we try to get to deeper levels of reality and at the same time have broader, more encompassing theories. Somehow I see theology at the core reflecting on the deepest experiences that we are capable of as humans and therefore also the most *relevant* to us from the human, personal point of view. Science would then be a reflection on the outer experiences. Using the tree as a metaphor, theology would deal with the roots and science with the branches.

Now, obviously there will be an overlap, because what is a deep level of reality and what is an outer level of reality can only be loosely defined. So there will be an interface. At that interface, science and religion traditionally got into trouble and now can inspire one another.

DAVID: Well, they did not always get into trouble traditionally. There were periods in history in which a particular religion was really carrying the whole scientific endeavor of the time. Islam in the Middle Ages is a case in point. Islam was strong in carrying science forward. Or just think of the many scientists that belonged to religious orders. In the Middle Ages the monks were the guardians of all academic knowledge for centuries; therefore the scientific knowledge of that time was also handed on by monks.

But let us talk about the present. What do you see as our common ground?

FRITJOF: I think the image of a wave, which you like to use, David, is a very apt one. The theologian and the scientist are like two corks floating on the same wave. The wave would be the collective consciousness, the culture, or the Zeitgeist, something like this. This collective consciousness is going through a change of paradigms, a groundswell, as it were. I think that is the common ground. It manifests itself in science, and it manifests itself in theology.

The manifestations of the change of paradigms may be summarized in the five criteria we established. Those are the parallels that we were pointing out.

DAVID: Our common ground is shifting ground.

FRITJOF: I could also say that the reason we can compare science to theology is that they are both paths toward an understanding of reality. They are paths that have great differences, but also have great similarities.

DAVID: How would you characterize them?

FRITJOF: The similarities are that both are based on experience and on a certain kind of systematic observation, so they are empirical. Of course, there are great differences in the way scientists and theologians observe. But our disciplines are both theoretical reflections on experience.

DAVID: That's helpful. Now, you are certainly not saying that science and theology are concerned with two different realms of reality but with one and the same realm from different aspects. Is that correct?

FRITJOF: First of all, I would say they are both concerned with human experience.

DAVID: So that's already one and the same realm.

FRITJOF: Yes, but then I would say that the theologian and the scientist are concerned with different kinds of human experience that overlap. Even if they didn't overlap, a comparison would be possible and interesting.

DAVID: But you say they do overlap.

FRITJOF: They do, so it's even more interesting.

DAVID: Science and theology could be regarded as interacting approaches to the same reality, namely, human experience. As conventional wisdom has it, science asks for the *how* and theology asks for the *why.*

FRITJOF: That's an interesting way of formulating it: Science asks for the *how* and theology, the *why.* I agree with that. But then the how and the why can not always be separated. Science asks for the how, more precisely for how a particular phenomenon is connected to all the other phenomena. If you include more and more connections, ultimately you will reveal the entire context, which is, in fact, the why. *Why* is connected with meaning, if you are defining meaning as context.

DAVID: Our context is how and why. Quite concretely, a scientist who studies how natural phenomena work might suddenly feel the question arising in his heart, Why are there natural phenomena? Why is there anything at all? This leads him to the religious horizon. A theologian, on the other hand, who professionally deals with that horizon of why, lives in a world in which she or he cannot survive without paying close attention also to everything that has to do with how this world works.

FRITJOF: I would say that scientific activity is motivated by a certain set of values. What I do as a scientist, whether I choose to go into this science or that science or, within a scientific field, to do one kind of research or another kind of research, is quite clearly a value decision. I do what I like better, what interests me more, what gives me more money, what gives me more status. All these decisions are based on a certain set of values. This set of values may or may not be spiritually grounded. If it is, then that would be an influence, not of theology proper, but certainly of spirituality on science. A spiritual scientist today—with a deep sense of belonging to the universe and valuing all that is in it—would not work, for example, in weapons research.

DAVID: This is a good example of the way a person's spirituality inevitably influences that person's stance in life, hence also one's stance as a scientist. And since one's spirituality is (partly at least) an expression of one's theology—of one's reflection on the basic God-experience—I'd say that, in this sense at least, theology has an influence on science.

FRITJOF: In the old days, of course, theology influenced science also in terms of the theories. Take for example Newton's idea that God, as he put it, "In the beginning formed matter in solid, massy, hard, impenetrable, movable particles." Such an influence is largely absent today, but in some scientists, I think, it is still present.

DAVID: Would you say that this is compatible with new thinking in science?

FRITJOF: What I'm saying is that a theology, or in a broader sense a religious perspective on the world, will in some cases influence the scientific theories. You remember we said that scientific theories describe all this interconnectedness, and then you arrive at a horizon where you can no longer describe it. But you want consistency among your fundamental beliefs in the meaning of it all, these fundamental questions that are religious questions. You want it to jibe with your religious experience, and I know scientists who want that. They want to be supported in pursuing their particular theory by their religious beliefs or by their religious experiences. This was very prevalent in the seventeenth century.

DAVID: But today, would this not affect our understanding of science and its goals? Wouldn't we discourage it?

FRITJOF: I don't know. It depends on what kind of influence we're talking about. That's a very difficult question. I'm thinking of this in a positive sense. For instance, I know scientists whose Buddhist practice is in perfect agreement with their scientific theories.

DAVID: "Perfect agreement," as you call it, is probably the goal that motivates our efforts to find the right relationship among all areas of our life. Science and theology are only two of those areas. We long for a worldview in which all the different areas agree with one another, perfectly, if possible. And since a new worldview is emerging in our time, both science and theology will have to express themselves in new ways.

2 The Methods of Science and Theology

FRITJOF: Well, let's talk about the ways science and theology express themselves, the methods that are characteristic of science and theology. We said that both are intellectual reflections on experience, and in both cases you gain knowledge. The result is knowledge about reality. In both science and theology you have a body of knowledge about reality. Now, what distinguishes science from the other paths to knowledge is a certain method.

The scientific method

FRITJOF: There are differences of opinion, I suppose, among scientists as to what constitutes the scientific method. I have decided for myself on two criteria. One is systematic observation; the other is the construction of a scientific model to represent the results of this observation. In past times systematic observation has often meant a controlled experiment, and that was very closely linked to the notion of dominating nature, controlling nature. Of course, there are sciences where you can't do this, like astronomy. You cannot control the stars, it's quite obvious. But you can do systematic observation. And the results of this systematic observation, the data, are then connected in a coherent way, in a way that is free of internal contradictions. The result is a representation of this data in something we call a model. Or, if it is more comprehensive, we call it a theory, but there is really no clear distinction between a model and a theory in contemporary scientific terminology.

A scientific model has two very important characteristics. One is its internal consistency: it has to be internally coherent, without contradictions. The other characteristic is that it is approximate, and that is very, very important from the contemporary scientific point of view. Whatever we say in science is a limited and approximate description of reality. Scientists, if you wish, do not deal with truth, if I mean by truth an exact correspondence between what is observed and the description of the observed phenomenon. Truth in that sense does not exist in science. Whatever we say is approximate. As Heisenberg says in *Physics and Philosophy*, "Every word or concept, clear as it may seem to be, has only a limited range of applicability."

And now I can throw that back to you two and ask how this works in theology. What is the method of theology?

The method of theology

THOMAS: Let me reflect on these two points—systematic observation and the building of models. Some recent theologians have adopted the model aspect of scientific methodology. One of them is Avery Dulles, an American Jesuit; another is Bernard Lonergan. But I personally tend to see the method of theology as very different from that of natural science. Not that the two methods are in opposition or conflict; they are just very different. One of the problems in the history of theology has been the assumption that theology is a science as Aristotle defined it: "the knowledge of things through their causes." The status of "science" was something that the medieval Scholastics, for instance, claimed for their own theological system. Contemporary theologians generally avoid making this claim. Theology is the *understanding* of faith or "faith in search of understanding," *fides quaerens intellectum*—that's the classical definition of theology. And as an understanding of a mystery, theology can not comprehend the total meaning of the mystery. Theological understanding is, to use an expression scientists often use, "approximate," or, as theologians prefer to say, it is "analogous"; that is, we affirm a certain similarity between God and all that we know through our senses and intellect while also affirming God's infinite otherness. God is always "similar" and always infinitely "different." This is something that any responsible theologian has to make clear: that however near our theology may come to knowing the ultimate mystery, it can never *comprehend* the mystery.

Faith

FRITJOF: You have now slipped in another word, *faith*. We talked about experience, about reflection on experience, religion, spirituality, but we haven't spoken about faith. What is faith?

THOMAS: It's hard to define faith in a few words. In a general sense, religious faith is a kind of knowledge and a kind of experience. Faith includes an element of surprise as well; it is an experience of reality that is surprising, yet it also rings true to our nature. In the biblical tradition and in Christianity, it's emphasized that faith as knowledge of God is a gift of God. However, faith is more than mere intellectual assent to information fed into our minds from outside, even if it comes from God. Faith includes God's self-disclosure within us and our response to God, which is fulfilled in love.

FRITJOF: The way I grew up, and the way probably most of us grew up, was to learn that doctrine is expressed as a series of dogmas, and faith is to believe that these dogmas are absolutely true.

DAVID: The word *faith* is used in many different ways, even within theology. One may mean doctrine, the "deposit of faith" toward which religious belief is directed. That is by no means the primary or most important aspect of faith at all. Faith is also used synonymously with belief. That's not primary either.

FRITJOF: So what is the real, the deepest meaning?

DAVID: Faith, I would say, is a matter of trust. Courageous trust in that ultimate belonging which you experience in your religious moments, in your peak moments. Faith is that inner gesture by which you entrust yourself to that belonging. The element of trust is primary. Faith is courageous trust in belonging. In our great moments, we experience that belonging. But it seems too good to be true, and so we cannot quite entrust ourselves to it. But when we do entrust ourselves to life, to the world, then our attitude is faith in the deepest sense. It's an inner gesture of the kind we mean when we speak of "having faith in someone" or of "acting in good faith."

FRITJOF: This exists also in science, interestingly enough. You know that every leap into novelty, every discovery, is an intuitive leap. But there are some scientists who are more intuitive than others. And the most highly intuitive scientists have this kind of faith. It's very typical of them that they somehow know it in their bones that this will lead them somewhere, and they can trust this intuition. Heisenberg, for instance, said that in the early 1920s, people slowly got "into the spirit" of quantum mechanics before they were able to formulate it, and that was a highly intuitive thing. And people like Niels Bohr, for instance, or Geoffrey Chew or Richard Feynman in physics—I know several of them—just sense that this is the way to go, that they will get somewhere. They have an insight, but they cannot talk about it yet, they cannot formulate it. So there is something like faith in science, too.

DAVID: Maybe the difference here is that this "faith," at least the way you have described it, is largely intellectual intuition.

FRITJOF: Well, if you call intuition intellectual.

DAVID: It has to do with knowing, that kind of trust. You have an intuition, a hunch. While the trust of faith, in the religious sense, is an existential trust. You can entrust your whole life to this.

FRITJOF: You see, the two are related. In science, too, there is a shadow of that existential aspect, because for a scientist, a theory to which you dedicate your life, your scientific career, has an existential quality. That faith has an existential quality, not in the broad sense, but it's more than intellectual.

DAVID: Maybe I should not have said "intellectual." What I meant is "noetic," the scientist's "faith" has to do with intuitive knowing, but it still moves on the level of knowing, not, for instance, on the level of morals at all. But religious faith also embraces morals and that ritual in everyday life which we called spirituality.

FRITJOF: But there are scientists, and I count myself among them, who want to make this connection now, reconnecting to morals.

DAVID: Now, here we have a very interesting point. I was hoping we would get to this. Are you now speaking as a scientist or as a human being who happens to be a scientist? I think when you speak about this broader connection which you just now mentioned, you are really speaking about yourself as a human being who also happens to be a scientist. And that puts the thing in perspective. Religious faith addresses the whole human being, as a human being, in the context of other human beings and of the whole cosmos. Scientific faith is a certain hunch that you're on the right track to figure out some question about the physical world, but it doesn't have any intrinsic connection with ultimate meaning or morality. Somebody working on developing chemical weapons may have remarkable scientific faith in the sense of a great intuitive sense of how to proceed.

FRITJOF: I agree. Now, Father Thomas, when you were saying that theology is the understanding of faith, what exactly did you mean?

THOMAS: To say that theology is the understanding of faith means that it is not the same as faith. It means making concrete sense of what we intuitively grasp in faith and applying that sense to the whole of our life. Theology is something that comes after faith, is at the service of faith, and is a way of increasing faith. Faith is something that has degrees. There is a qualitative expansion of development of faith in the believer and in the community of faith. Theology serves to make faith grow as a social reality, as a social experience.

FRITJOF: But it also leads to a body of knowledge. That's what it has in common with science.

Theological models

DAVID: This may be the point where we can start developing the parallel. I would start from the model making. I think it would be justified to say that theology is a human effort to make models that spring from our knowledge and exploration of the religious experience in the widest sense. Definitely, theological models, too, must be internally consistent. Sometimes they are not, and that calls for development and new models. Or we found them consistent in the past but no longer find them so. That leads to a paradigm shift, exactly as in science.

Then theological models, too, are only approximate. That is sometimes difficult for people to accept who invest so much effort in theology, and for church leaders who identify fidelity with adherence to particular models of faith. You know how difficult it is in science to remember that models are only approximate. When people are existentially as engaged as they are in theology, they tend to equate these insights with the whole truth.

FRITJOF: I think it's very important to see that the notion of approximation is much more difficult in theology because of the existential engagement. The personal engagement of scientists can be pretty strong, too, but it's a different matter when you're existentially engaged, when your salvation depends on it.

DAVID: Salvation in the sense of realizing your connection to the whole, of real belonging; that is salvation. And salvation really means realizing your connection to the whole of the universe, your experience of being at home, feeling secure, truly belonging in some ultimate sense. Your finding your place in the cosmos depends on it, and so you tend to forget that it is only approximate.

Revelation

FRITJOF: Now, what is revelation? Would that be what David calls our finest moments?

THOMAS: Revelation doesn't have one consistent theological definition. Until recently the dominant theological paradigm emphasized revelation as God disclosing a certain body of knowledge that we couldn't attain on our own. Today the emphasis is more on revelation as a history of salvation, as an ongoing historical process in which God's nature and purpose are disclosed in interaction with those who believe in God. Revelation cannot be understood if it's broken up into bits and pieces. It has to be taken as a whole.

FRITJOF: Let me rephrase the question. You said before that science and theology were really very different, but we have established a lot of commonality now. One area in which they may be different is revelation. In science we have systematic observation and then we have model building. And in theology there is revelation.

DAVID: Let me try that. We spoke about this sense of belonging. All the religions of the world would admit that this is our basic common ground. This is the experiential ground. So we have now established something that we could call God, if you want to use that term for the reference point of our ultimate belonging. God is the one to whom we ultimately belong.

Expressed in this way, this insight presupposes a long journey of exploration into God. It already presupposes the recognition that the reference point of our belonging must be personal. If I am personal, then the one to whom I belong must be personal. But of course God must not be restricted by any of the limitations we associate with being a person. One of those limitations is, for instance, that being me, I cannot at the same time be another. This does not apply to God. In other words, God must have all the perfection of being a person and none of the limitations.

Now, from there, it is again a long journey of exploration until we come to see that God freely allows us to belong, gives us this belonging. Up to this point, it was a sort of territory I was exploring, God-territory. But now all of a sudden I experience Yes! I am doing the exploring, but it isn't just my exploring, it is at the same time God's unveiling Godself. In the process of religious history, which stretches over millennia, this is a milestone. Yet every one of us can relive this experience. To explore into God is prayer, not in the conventional sense, but in the sense that theology is prayer. As we explore the God-territory prayerfully, we suddenly reach a point where we discover that it gives itself to us. God and the whole universe are giving themselves continuously to us.

FRITJOF: So revelation, then, is really connected with the notion of the personal God?

DAVID: Yes. I do not think that the term *revelation* could make any sense except in that context.

THOMAS: What I would add to this, to narrow it down a little bit, is a footnote on what specifically in the biblical tradition is seen as revelation. In the Bible, revelation is an intervention of God in human history, in the human situation. Revelation and salvation are inseparable. The Old Testament speaks of the living God who intervenes in the situation of an alienated, oppressed people and brings them out of their slavery. In other words, we discover that now at last we are not alienated, in that we know God. And we know God by being saved.

DAVID: It's a living process, but I wanted to catch you on "God intervening," because we often use this term and forget that it is a storytelling way of talking about revelation. God doesn't sit up there and then intervene occasionally. It's not so much an intervention on God's part as a discovery, a liberation, a new insight on our part.

THOMAS: We know who God is because we have the experience of being freed from our alienation. Of course, we don't need to use the term *intervene.*

FRITJOF: This reminds me of the Buddhist and Hindu notion of remembering who we really are. For instance, the Zen koan says, "What was your face before you were conceived?" And in the Hindu tradition you have the myth of God creating the world and then forgetting who he is. And since we are that creation, the liberation, the *moksha,* is to remember that we are actually God. *Tat tvam asi.* That, I think, one could call revelation. If I remember my true nature in meditation and rediscover my divine nature, then something is revealed to me by my deeper self. Couldn't you say that?

DAVID: Since God is the self of ourselves, truth is always revealed by our deeper self. But I would be careful in using the term *revelation* too broadly. My emphasis when I speak of revelation falls on God's self-revealing. The correct image is not that of your pulling away a veil but of the bride unveiling herself for the bridegroom. That is the underlying image of revelation. Therefore it comes close to Heidegger's notion of truth, connected with the Greek word for truth.

THOMAS: That word is *alētheia*, which means "unhiddenness": the truth deliberately "unhides" itself, lights itself up. This is something we all experience.

DAVID: Hinduism, for example, includes theistic traditions. I would not hesitate to speak of revelation there. But what is so much more important to me than revelation in this or that historic tradition is that it is part of our own experience. Revelation is not just some objective information that is given to us out there. It is a personal discovery of relatedness, of intimately, essentially belonging to the source of everything.

FRITJOF: Now, when you defined theology as an understanding of faith, that would be an understanding through intellectual exploration *and*, I suppose, through revelation. Would you say so?

THOMAS: Yes. Faith is this kind of total self-giving to revelation, or to God who reveals himself by saving me and by revealing to me my true self. I think the sequence is, first revelation, then faith as a response, and finally a moment of understanding; the understanding of faith is necessary in order both to relive that moment, the fundamental meeting with reality, and to communicate it to others.

FRITJOF: So revelation is really the basis of your faith then.

THOMAS: Revelation is the basis. Faith can be understood as *response* to revelation, a welcoming, an embracing.

FRITJOF: And then theology is the intellectual exploration of that response. I think you could say that what we talked about earlier is the experience of belonging from *our* point of view. But if you belong to somebody, there is also the other point of view. And that would be revelation.

DAVID: That is the key word. There is a key word in the Psalms that seems to me to be one of those milestones of discovery: "O God, you are my God." O God, you are *my* God, you *belong* to me!

FRITJOF: So the belonging is a two-way street.

DAVID: A two-way street! That is the tremendous discovery.

FRITJOF: And that would be different from science.

DAVID: Yes, but it is obviously something that scientists can enter into and understand as human beings, but not as scientists, because science is not *concerned* with this matter.

FRITJOF: Then, again, there is a very important difference here with the kind of science that we want to overcome. Ever since Francis Bacon, the aim of most scientists has been the domination of nature and the exploitation of nature. Bacon used these very vicious metaphors of seeing nature as a woman, and what you do as a scientist is torture her secrets out of her. This is clearly not revelation. It's the very opposite. It's rape, actually. Now, when it filters down to the everyday life of the scientist, there is still a great difference between science and theology, because science is active exploring, not sitting there in prayer or meditation and allowing reality to reveal itself. Nevertheless, the whole attitude in science has been what Schumacher called a science of manipulation rather than a science of wisdom. What we want to recapture now is the science of wisdom, and maybe revelation will play a great role there.

DAVID: At least in Heidegger's sense that reality gives itself, unveils itself to us *deliberately.* And we are awestruck with this gift. It is available to everybody, to every human being. That is the main thing, the world gives itself to us. It gives itself freely to us, if we just allow it. It showers us with gifts.

Scientific discipline/spiritual discipline

DAVID: When Fritjof spoke about method in science, he first spoke about systematic observation, which then leads to model building. With regard to building models, we have a perfect parallel in theology —internal consistency and approximation. But what would correspond to systematic observation?

FRITJOF: I think that would be prayer, quite clearly. It is systematic, and if you're serious about it, you start at four in the morning, like you do in your tradition.

DAVID: Yes, meditation and prayer in the widest sense, and in fact the whole tradition of spiritual discipline or asceticism.

FRITJOF: How do you understand asceticism?

DAVID: As practices which help to prepare oneself for religious experience. Various meditation experiences, for example. Or fasting, which is gaining new popularity today. Or simply the cultivation of a sense of gratefulness in one's life, gratefulness for colors and sounds and smells and textures. Here the goal is to make one more alive by making the senses more alive.

FRITJOF: In a way this really corresponds to systematic observation in science, because it is also systematic. It's a practice. The root of the word *ascetic,* the Greek *askēsis,* means to practice gymnastics. So asceticism is a practice with the goal of leading to religious experiences.

DAVID: Well, we have to be careful with the expression "leading to" religious experiences. Asceticism as such is something that is highly recommendable for theologians, but asceticism is not part of the discipline of theology, except that there is a theology *of* asceticism, ascetic theology.

FRITJOF: Asceticism is part of the religious experience, though.

DAVID: It doesn't bring about the religious experience, but it leaves you open for it. It prepares you for it. God's revelation, the breaking through of the divine reality into our everyday reality, is something that is going on continuously. By making ourselves more perceptive to it, we receive it. These various practices of making yourself perceptive are asceticism.

FRITJOF: If I compare this to my work as a physicist, I would say, "There are photons and neutrinos in our room all the time. But we can't see them with our eyes. But if I bring in my apparatus plus my ten years of training to use the apparatus and understand the signals, then I can observe them."

DAVID: This looks to me like a valid parallel. Some ascetics stress so much the negative aspect of their methods that for many people asceticism has come to mean "abstain from this," "abstain from that," "cut down on sleep," "fast," and so forth. Our particular Benedictine tradition stresses, more than many others, the positive aspects: sharpening the senses, gratefulness, mindfulness.

FRITJOF: In the Buddhist tradition I understand that this corresponds to the Eightfold Path: "right seeing," "right speech," "right livelihood," and so on. This is a Buddhist discipline, which also has moral aspects.

DAVID: The Eightfold Path has strong moral overtones. Asceticism seems to be the side of our moral life that is turned toward the mystic experience, while another side of the moral life is turned toward social interaction. That is the side we most properly call morals; the other side we call asceticism.

FRITJOF: I'm also thinking of Castaneda and his notion of the way of the warrior. I would compare that to asceticism. It's a certain moral attitude of not clinging to things, doing things as well as you can, and then not worrying about the outcome; living in the present. Castaneda uses this powerful metaphor of death being always at your side to talk about mindfulness.

DAVID: And that is really what asceticism is all about: being in the present moment mindfully and gratefully. That is my key concern. One reason why we have to cut down is that we are so swamped with things that we can not pay proper attention to them. For instance, in fasting: We are so surfeited with food that we can not really eat a piece of bread gratefully. We have too much. So in order to make ourselves mindful, we have to fast and then eat this one piece of bread and really focus on it.

FRITJOF: That is like the experimental method in science. You don't observe all of nature. You take out one plant and then you don't even observe the entire plant. You observe only one leaf. The danger in science has been reductionism. You go to smaller and smaller parts, and you forget the whole.

DAVID: You forget why you are doing it.

FRITJOF: You forget why you are doing it, and you also forget the function of the part in the whole. Then you try to build up the whole from the parts, and it doesn't work. This is why we need this shift from the parts to the whole now.

DAVID: And there is a parallel to that in asceticism. You start out by limiting yourself so as to become fully alive, and then since limiting costs you a certain effort, you put so much emphasis on the limiting, on the negative, on the cutting off and throwing out, that this becomes an end in itself. In science as well as in asceticism there is always the danger of missing the forest for the trees.

THOMAS: In spiritual practice in general—and asceticism in particular —the goal is always the recovery of wholeness. Today, I believe, the attainment of this goal requires great discretion in the use of physical means such as fasting and sleep deprivation. We need to recover, after thirteen centuries of Platonic dualism and three centuries of Cartesian dualism, a profoundly holistic understanding of ourselves as embodied spirit in the world, part of this world of bodies and open to Absolute Spirit or God.

3 Paradigms in Science and Theology

Paradigms in science and society

FRITJOF: We have talked about the purposes and the methods of science and theology. Now I would like to introduce a historical perspective and talk about how scientific theories develop and how knowledge is accumulated in science. As you know, until recently the belief was that there is a steady accumulation of knowledge; that theories gradually get more and more comprehensive and more and more accurate.

Thomas Kuhn introduced the idea of paradigms and paradigm shifts, which says there are these periods of steady accumulation, which he calls normal science, but then there are periods of scientific revolutions where the paradigm changes. A scientific paradigm, according to Kuhn, is a constellation of achievements—by that he means concepts, values, techniques, and so on—shared by a scientific community and used by that community to define legitimate problems and solutions.

So this means that behind the scientific theory is a certain framework within which science is pursued. And it's important to notice that this framework includes not just concepts but also values and techniques. So the activity of doing science is part of the paradigm. The attitude of domination and control, for example, is part of a scientific paradigm.

DAVID: Would you say it is part of the paradigm? Or is it a force that conditions the paradigm?

FRITJOF: It is part of the paradigm, because it's part of the values underlying the scientific theories. The values are part of the paradigm. So a paradigm to Kuhn and to me is more than a worldview, more than a conceptual framework, because it includes values and activities. To make this clearer, let me show you how I enlarged that, following Marilyn Ferguson and Willis Harman and other people who have often used "paradigm" in a larger sense. I have taken the Kuhnian definition and enlarged it to that of a social paradigm.

A social paradigm, for me, is a constellation of concepts, values, perceptions, and practices, shared by a community that forms a particular vision of reality that is the basis of the way the community organizes itself. It's necessary for a paradigm to be shared by a community. A single person can have a worldview, but a paradigm is shared by a community.

DAVID: And why do you speak only about communal organization and not about the whole life of the community? Why do you focus on the organization only? Why not on values?

FRITJOF: I have not explored the difference between paradigm and culture. You could say the basis of the whole life is the culture. The two are closely related, but I have not gone into this.

Now Kuhn, of course, uses the term in a narrower sense, and within science he talks about different paradigms. I use it in a very broad sense, the sort of overarching paradigm underlying the organization of a certain society or the organization of science in a certain scientific community.

DAVID: I asked about values because I thought you were still talking about a paradigm shift within a particular science. There the values would of course be implicit, not at all explicit.

FRITJOF: The entire notion of the paradigm is implicit in the periods of normal science, and it's very difficult to delineate the paradigm and to show where its limitations are, where its borders are. It's only in times when the paradigm changes that you see its limitations, and, in fact, it changes *because* of these limitations. Kuhn has written very extensively about that. When there are problems, which he calls anomalies, that can no longer be solved within the dominant paradigm, these shifts occur. And of course it takes a while until these problems actually force people to shift.

In physics, for example, the most recent paradigm shift began in the 1920s when various problems connected with atomic structure could not be solved in terms of Newtonian science. And what I am saying in my book *The Turning Point* is that now we are in a situation in society where the social paradigm has reached its limitations. These limitations are the threat of nuclear war, the devastation of our natural environment, the persistence of poverty around the world—all these very severe problems that can no longer be solved in the old paradigm.

Kuhn, by the way, speaks of a pre-paradigmatic period where there are competing views. One of them will then become the dominant paradigm, shared by the scientific community. In society or, say, in the human family, this is different, because we do have different coexisting social paradigms. The Islamic social paradigm is different from the Japanese or from the American. So the same group of phenomena—like economics, politics, and social life—will be understood in terms of different coexisting paradigms.

DAVID: Can you explain why different paradigms can coexist in a social context and not in science?

FRITJOF: There *could* be different coexisting paradigms also in science, and there were in the past, but not since the rise of European science in the seventeenth century. Wherever people do science now, in the modern sense of the term, they would do science according to the European paradigm, whether it's in Japan or China or Africa. Many scientists say they have been brainwashed to do that. They could do science within another paradigm, but they don't. There is a certain colonialization of scientists by European and American science. Now it's America, but the roots, of course, are in European science. Whereas in social matters, there's not nearly so much dominance of a single paradigm. Different cultures coexist. In science we do not find different cultures coexisting; there's basically one scientific culture.

DAVID: What you said just now is really very important, yet it often goes unnoticed that even in science it would be possible to have different paradigms next to one another. It is almost accidental that there is one scientific paradigm, due to the colonialism of Western science. It need not be so. You said that scientists could do science in a different paradigm. This is important. However, people often say, "Well, this is just the strength of science, that it unifies. In science there can be no contradictions. Science is the rock-bottom basis for all truth," and so on.

FRITJOF: But you see, science is pursued within the larger paradigm. So, for instance, if two scientific groups worked on the Strategic Defense Initiative (SDI) project, they would get very similar results. They would construct laser beams for use in outer space, space stations, killer satellites, and so on. Although the results would differ somewhat, as they do in science when it is done in different countries, more or less the same conclusions would be reached. But you could easily imagine that in one culture it would be absolutely out of the question even to work on such a project, because the values would be different.

DAVID: That's what I want to emphasize, the connection between the social and the scientific paradigm: what kind of a society we live in determines what kind of a science we are going to have.

FRITJOF: Yes, the scientific paradigm is embedded in the social paradigm.

DAVID: Much more so than people realize. Now, let me ask you something else. I have long been fascinated with the concept of ether. Ether played such an important role in the history of science up to the late nineteenth century at least. Now it has been dropped completely. What happened? Why was it needed, and why is it not needed anymore? Maybe we can find a parallel here with certain theological concepts that also seemed urgently needed at one time and are now no longer necessary. That seems to be a typical phenomenon in times of paradigm changes.

FRITJOF: Yes, it is. This phenomenon of concepts that are needed during a time and then are not needed anymore happens again and again in science. We build models and then we discard them, because we have better models. Then finally we have a complete theory that is not discarded. It will be superseded by better theories but will still be valid within its range of applicability.

Among the scientific concepts that were discarded when a new model was adopted, the ether is perhaps the most famous, and rightly so, because the shift of perceptions that allowed us to discard the concept of an ether marks the beginning of twentieth-century physics.

This is a fascinating subject. It begins with the question of the nature of light, and it is a very powerful illustration of the fact that such an everyday experience as sunlight reaching the Earth is something that goes beyond our powers of imagination. We have no way to imagine how sunlight reaches the Earth. Although people normally are unaware of this, this question got scientists into modern physics.

In the nineteenth century, Michael Faraday and Clerk Maxwell developed a comprehensive theory of electromagnetism, which culminated in the discovery that light consists of rapidly alternating electric and magnetic fields that travel through space as waves. These fields are nonmechanical entities, and Maxwell's equations, which describe their exact behavior, were the first theory that went beyond Newtonian mechanics. That was the great triumph of nineteenth-century physics.

However, when Maxwell made his discovery, he was immediately faced with a problem. If light consists of electromagnetic waves, how can these waves travel through empty space? We know from our experience and from the theory of waves that every wave needs a medium. A water wave needs the water that is disturbed and then moves up and down as the wave passes through. A sound wave needs the particles of air, vibrating as the wave passes through. Without air or some other material substance, there is no sound. But light waves travel through empty space, where there is no medium to transmit the vibrations. So what is vibrating in a light wave?

This is what led scientists to invent the ether. They said, "There's no air, but there is an invisible medium, called ether, in which light waves travel." This ether had to have fancy properties. For example, it had to be a weightless and perfectly elastic substance. You see, when water waves travel, they diminish because of friction, but light waves don't. So the ether had to be perfectly elastic without any friction. Scientists at the beginning of the twentieth century could not bring themselves to abandon the notion of an ether, in spite of its strange properties, because this mechanistic image of a wave needing a medium was so firmly ingrained in their minds.

It took an Einstein to say that there was no ether, that light is a physical phenomenon in its own right, which doesn't need a medium. It doesn't need a medium, said Einstein, because it manifests not only as waves but also as particles, which can travel through empty space. He called those particles of light quanta, which gave the name to quantum theory, the theory of atomic phenomena.

The struggle with the question, In what sense exactly is a quantum of light a particle and in what sense is it a wave? is the story of quantum theory, spanning the first three decades of the century. At the end of that exciting period, physicists understood that light waves are really "probability waves"—that is, abstract mathematical patterns that give you the probability of finding a particle of light (which today we call photon) in a particular place when you look for it. These probability patterns are wave patterns that travel through empty space. So, without going into further details, the end of the story is that light is both particles and waves, and the ether is no longer needed.

DAVID: So in physics we once had a concept that seemed absolutely indispensable, and then it dropped away. I think there are parallels to this phenomenon in theology.

THOMAS: The classic example of an unnecessary doctrine within common Christian theological thought is the geocentric universe. In order to uphold the truthfulness of the Bible, medieval theologians thought it necessary to posit an immobile Earth at the center of a moving cosmos. During the Renaissance, Copernicus and others elaborated another theory: that the Earth is not the center but is moving around the sun. Galileo sustained the Copernican thesis. At the same time, however, Galileo was an ardent Catholic who desired to remain in full communion with the Christian Church. He was not unsophisticated in theology. He had read the Bible and felt the need to explain the relationship between science and theology, or better yet, between scientific language and biblical language.

FRITJOF: What was the theological problem?

THOMAS: Theologians believed that since the Bible said, "The sun stood still," for instance, it was necessary, in order not to cast doubt on the truth of Holy Scripture, to assume that the sun moved around the Earth.

DAVID: One mistook poetic language for scientific reporting.

THOMAS: Galileo said that this verse of the Bible, "The sun stood still," was a religious statement. The language it uses is the language of the common people; it addresses the masses, while science is for people who speak a different, more sophisticated language, the language of mathematics. The purpose of science is not to fulfill people's religious needs but to gain knowledge about the universe and to build the great edifice of empirical knowledge. This statement, with greater refinement, is one that any biblical scholar would make today.

FRITJOF: So what was the concept that was no longer needed?

THOMAS: The concept that was no longer needed was that of the immobile Earth. Ultimately theologians came to the conclusion that the Bible was not a scientific textbook, a source of answers to our questions about the physical universe.

FRITJOF: Could one say that the Bible speaks in terms of metaphors and models as we do in science? The metaphors of the Bible point toward religious truth, but they are not the full truth. So the metaphor should not be confused with the truth toward which the metaphor points.

THOMAS: Truth should never be confused with any of the ways we express truth, whether metaphorical or conceptual. That is why a number of theologians have adopted a "models" method typical of the natural sciences. I have already mentioned Avery Dulles and Bernard Lonergan, both of whom have made good use of this method (think of Dulles's *Models of the Church,* for instance). In the other Christian churches there are scholars like Ian Barbour and Langdon Gilkey. I think that the use of models in theology simply reflects the traditional awareness of the analogical character of all theological language. All we say about God is *analogy*—that is, whatever we affirm about God also implies God's infinite difference from everything else we know.

DAVID: Another concept that has become obsolete in more recent years is that of limbo. To many people, limbo was a much more burning issue than the geocentric universe. It was the idea that children who died unbaptized couldn't go to heaven, because they had original sin. One couldn't assign them to hell, so one invented limbo, an intermediate state. That caused tremendous sadness to many parents whose children died before baptism.

THOMAS: The doctrine of limbo was a theological conclusion from a hypothesis of Saint Augustine. Augustine conceived of original sin as original *guilt,* transmitted at conception to each human individual. Hence all of humanity is a *massa damnata,* an accursed mass, redeemed by Christ but still subject to sin; even the act of conceiving a child, the sex act, is for Augustine at least minimally sinful. Augustine's is only one possible solution to the theological issue of human propensity to sin, but his solution prevailed because of his exceptional importance in Western theology. So on the basis of Augustine's doctrine of the original guilt transmitted to each individual descendant of Adam and Eve, theologians elaborated the concept of limbo.

FRITJOF: So limbo was a realm that was neither heaven nor hell?

THOMAS: A realm that was neither heaven nor hell nor purgatory, but a place of eternal distance from God. There is no vision of God in limbo. Saint Augustine said that the children who died in original sin were not really tormented, but they did have to suffer "very gentle punishments." This rather absurd notion insinuated itself into the Catholic mentality and the common theological texts and came to be thought of as a certain doctrine, when in fact it was not.

FRITJOF: How was it resolved?

THOMAS: It was resolved by a greater knowledge of the historical background of this teaching, confined to a certain current of Western Christian thought. In fact, the Orthodox tradition of the Christian East posits a very different understanding of original sin, which does not necessarily include the notion of transmitted guilt and therefore does not see humanity as an accursed mass; infants, sharing in the human nature of Christ, will be taken up into his presence if they die before baptism and before the age of reason.

FRITJOF: So what then is the new-paradigm interpretation?

THOMAS: The new-paradigm theology does not even bother to interpret the concept of limbo; it has discarded it.

FRITJOF: Right. But how does it interpret original sin?

THOMAS: That is a very delicate and difficult point, because the content of the Catholic doctrine is not entirely clear, other than the recognition that our nature is deeply wounded—something of which we are all aware—and that we are in absolute need of grace for salvation.

FRITJOF: Then the problem is not solved?

THOMAS: The problem is not solved. It's one of those areas where there is a certain space for theological discussion.

DAVID: When an educated person in the West asks me, "What is original sin?" I answer that it is the Christian term for the universal phenomenon the Buddhists call *dukkha*. The original meaning of that term refers to a wheel that grinds on its axle: Something is out of order. I choose the Buddhist notion of *dukkha* because even in the West many people have a better understanding of *dukkha* than of "original sin." Both concepts arise from the acknowledgment that something is wrong with existence. Human life "grinds on its axle," as it were. Not only the

Buddhist and the Christian but every religious tradition starts with this recognition that something is out of order with us, that we are lost and have to find our way home.

FRITJOF: And in children this kind of condition is not even developed. The full human condition is not developed in a small child.

DAVID: But children are born into this condition, because our society is out of whack. The stress on the social aspects of original sin, on societal distortions, is much stronger in theology today than it used to be. That corresponds much more closely to the original Biblical notion of what we've come to call original sin.

THOMAS: Your mentioning the social conditions that are both effect and cause of sin leads me to the issue of the scientist's moral dilemma. If we can do a thing, does that necessarily mean we should? In the name of progress, our impulse was always to say, "Yes, go ahead." But is there any boundary, at least a theoretical one? If no boundary exists, how can we best protect ourselves and the planet? How can we equip ourselves spiritually to deal with the fruits of our own intellect?

FRITJOF: I think it is a very widespread misconception that there are no boundaries in science that would shield us from acquiring intellectual knowledge. The popular image is that of a scientist sitting in his lab, fascinated by some problem, and pursuing it regardless of the consequences. Intellectual curiosity, it is said, is a basic human characteristic, and as human beings we should have the right to follow that basic human curiosity.

Well, that image is totally false. That's not how science is done today at all. There *are* boundaries to human curiosity. In fact, there are two kinds of boundaries. The first boundary is that research is being pursued within the context of a larger paradigm that contains a certain set of values. What is interesting to a scientist is determined in part by those values. It is determined, of course, by personal predilection, but it is also determined by the paradigm. For example, to strap an animal into some mechanical contraption, torture it, and measure its pain thresholds is not intellectually exciting for me. To pour toxic substances in its eyes and measure the effect on the retina is not something I find interesting or rewarding. It is not attractive, because I don't operate within a paradigm that encourages that kind of research. So it's not that I say, "I shouldn't do that. But boy, would I like to. If I were allowed to, wouldn't that be something." Not at all. Just the opposite. I find this kind of research so repulsive that there's no intellectual excitement in it for me. In a different paradigm—and, of course, you know thousands of scientists do that kind of research—in a different kind of paradigm all sorts of arguments could be found to make this exciting or at least interesting research. This is an extreme example. But I think that in most scientific endeavors, the research question will fall within or outside the paradigm as far as its values are concerned, and the things that don't lie within the paradigm are not likely to be exciting. That's one of the boundaries.

The second boundary is not an intellectual boundary but an economic, or financial, boundary. Today scientists who sit in their labs doing what they think is most exciting are very, very rare, if not nonexistent. Typically what happens is that you do research on a project that is funded. If you don't get the funds, you can't do the research. In order to get the funds, you write grant proposals, and you formulate these grant proposals in the language of the dominant paradigm if you want to get money. Otherwise you won't. This is where the values come in socially. So what you can pursue in your research depends on what gets funded.

THOMAS: Would you also say that the underlying idea of seeking knowledge in this Faustian or Promethean way is also part of the old paradigm? In other words, seeking to amass knowledge in order to gain power over nature?

FRITJOF: Absolutely. It's not only part of the old paradigm; it doesn't even recognize the existence of paradigms. It recognizes neither that knowledge does not just accumulate nor that knowledge arises from a constellation of concepts, perceptions, values, and practices from which it cannot be separated.

DAVID: Speaking of funding, is it not in general rather difficult to get funding for interdisciplinary ventures?

FRITJOF: Absolutely.

DAVID: And isn't that also a sign that the new-paradigm thinking that favors interdisciplinary work has not yet seeped in?

FRITJOF: Yes, absolutely. It has not seeped into the grant–giving bodies at all. Most of the research that is funded today, not surprisingly, is military related. Over 75 percent of the so-called R & D money in America is funded by the military. This is, of course, a tremendous perversion of the scientific enterprise. The whole spirit of science is being distorted, and the scientific and engineering skills of a vast number of scientists are directed away from useful activity. Military research is waste almost by definition.

DAVID: Would you have some positive suggestions on how one could get out of this?

FRITJOF: You can not change the fact that scientific research is determined to a large part by the value system. The motivation to do one kind of research rather than another is determined by values. This value system, of course, may change. That's what the whole paradigm shift is about. The other part is that research is determined by what gets funded, and the funding of science should be democratized. Today it is not proceeding democratically. Ordinary citizens have very little input. If scientific research were funded more democratically, its direction would reflect the will of the community more. But this will happen only with a revitalization of the whole democratic process, with decentralization of economic and political power, and so on. This is what the Green movement in Europe has been pursuing with quite a bit of success.

DAVID: That sounds to me like a promising route to pursue in this country as well.

Paradigms in theology

FRITJOF: Now the question I would have regarding theology: Is there such a thing as a paradigm and a paradigm shift in theology? If so, what are the limitations of the current old paradigm in theology and why need there be new–paradigm thinking in theology?

THOMAS: If you ask whether different paradigms are legitimate in theology, the answer is yes, even in the most orthodox Christian tradition. They are legitimate because of the very nature of the object of theology, which is God as the ultimate mystery in which we are immersed but which we can never comprehend. Authentic theology has never claimed to resolve the mystery or reduce it to Descartes's "clear and distinct concepts." So a plurality of theological paradigms is both an inner necessity of the faith and a historical fact. Mainstream Christianity embraces at least four or more great eras of theologizing, each with its own internal consistency and rules, and yet with significant differences among them. Early Christianity generated several great theological currents in the various "apostolic" churches—Rome, Alexandria, Antioch, and, later, Constantinople. Medieval theology in the West evolved into the great synthesis of Christian and Aristotelian thought called Scholasticism. The Catholic response to the Protestant Reformation produced still another theological paradigm.

DAVID: I would say a paradigm shift in theology comes about to a lesser degree when the internal consistency of which you spoke is in question, when there are statements made that do not seem to fit with one another anymore. That leads to a minor shift, something has to be adjusted.

FRITJOF: But one could change the model within the same paradigm. It's the major anomalies that would usually give rise to changes of paradigms.

THOMAS: The problem might exist with regard to finding within theology an *exact* equivalent of the anomalies in science. I wonder whether we have that. A parallel to an anomaly could be what are called heresies, the challenge to the community's orthodoxy. Another could simply be the introduction of a new cultural input. I'm thinking, for example, of Aristotle's metaphysics and the commentaries on Aristotle by the Muslim thinkers, which theologians were beginning to read at the time of Thomas Aquinas in the thirteenth century. So I don't think we have an exact equivalent. Both the challenge of heresy and the contact with other cultures have a positive effect on theology; there's no question that the so-called heretics have sometimes contributed enormously to the final sifting out of what really is the community's faith.

DAVID: You are right. And the parallels to the paradigm shifts in science may be closer than we realize. Those people whom the establishment

ment branded as heretics challenged the then-prevailing paradigm of faith, religious practice, and theology in light of their own religious experience. That's not so different from a new cultural input confronting an aging paradigm. Today the old scientific paradigm is challenged by new human insights; for instance, by a new respect for our planet, which challenges scientists to face their responsibility for our environment. Science, in turn, can lead to a new human awareness by showing, for instance, how everything is connected with everything. The closer we feel related to animals, the more sensitive we become to the atrocities inflicted on animals by frivolous research and cold business interests in animal husbandry. Hence the protests: new thinking always challenges the "establishment," be it in theology or in science.

FRITJOF: For example, when we say, within the new social paradigm, that national security is an outdated concept, that statement runs counter to our national policies; it runs counter to the establishment. Similarly when Galileo said the planets have moons and the Earth goes around the sun, that affirmation ran counter to the establishment of his time. The difference, of course, is that then the establishment was the Church, and the dominant paradigm was the Aristotelian, Scholastic paradigm, while today the dominant paradigm is carried no longer by the Church but by the corporations and the mass media they own, by the government and military bureaucracies, and so on.

DAVID: Do we agree then that there is a paradigm shift in theology that is comparable to that in science?

THOMAS: I certainly agree that there's a paradigm shift in theology today, but whether and to what extent it is really comparable to the one in science is still not clear to me.

History of Christian paradigms

FRITJOF: In science, in order to sustain the development, whether it's the gradual development in the periods of normal science or the revolutionary development in periods of paradigm shifts, you have to continually do this systematic observation that is part of the scientific method. It would seem that in theology, if you want to refine your dogmas and your understanding of faith, the reflection on religious experience, you would also have to rely on continual religious experience. Now, as far as I can see, this is not the case today. And maybe I could even make a stronger statement and say that in Christianity this was never a strong point. The mystics were always sort of marginalized and often persecuted.

THOMAS: I think you have to nuance this with regard to the different epochs of what we're calling paradigms in Christian theology.

FRITJOF: Could you give us a short summary of these paradigms?

THOMAS: During the first thousand years of Christianity, it was generally recognized that theology had to be the fruit not only of a profound intellectual conviction but above all of an intense personal experience of the faith. This was the epoch of the "Fathers" of the Church—excuse the sexist language, but practically all the early Christian writers were men! There is hardly one of these Fathers whom you wouldn't also call a mystic: think of Origen and Gregory of Nyssa and Gregory Nazianzen in the East, Ambrose and Augustine and Pope Gregory the Great in the West.

The crisis of mysticism and deep religious experience in Christianity coincides with the emergence of the great scholastic paradigm. This was the period of Thomas Aquinas and Bonaventure in the thirteenth century, and the energy, you might say, of the Scholastic paradigm continued on into the sixteenth century; at that time you still had someone like Cajetan, who was a great commentator on Thomas Aquinas and also an original thinker. But what happened throughout this period was the progressive fragmentation of the theological discipline. First, Church law was divorced from theology, and then dogmatic theology, moral theology, and ascetical or spiritual theology each went its separate way. And finally dogmatic theology itself was broken down into specific "treatises." Progressive fragmentation was the price paid for a new systematic presentation of Christianity in terms of Aristotelian thought. From that time, there has been a constant tension between the theologian as the professional scholar of the contents of Christian teaching and the spiritual person who is trying to live this teaching on a deep level of practice and experience.

DAVID: Are you saying that, roughly, before the thirteenth century, the mystics were the theologians, and vice versa?

THOMAS: Certainly, in principle at least, it was axiomatic that the two were inseparable. And the attitude of the theologian was first of all that of a listener, a person of faith who is searching for adequate ways to explain the Christian experience and connect it with other knowledge. This is theology as *fides quaerens intellectum*, "faith seeking understanding." What is remarkable about early Christian thought is that both the orthodox Fathers and the "heretics" had basically the same view of theology's purpose: to initiate the believer into a genuine *gnosis,* an experiential knowledge of God. Not a purely intellectual knowledge, but one that totally transforms and, as many early writers say, "divinizes" the believer.

FRITJOF: And from the thirteenth century on, you were saying, there was this tension between the theologians on the one hand and the mystics on the other.

THOMAS: It was the paradigm itself that imposed this division and almost forbade the theologian to become too mystical. He had to remain on the intellectual level. Let me add, though, that the crisis of mysticism was something that happened largely in the West. The Eastern Church continued, for the most part, in the line of holistic theology. But by then the two churches had excommunicated each other.

FRITJOF: This makes it, of course, very difficult for this whole parallel between science and theology. If religious experience has not been the ground of theology in the theological establishment for the past seven centuries, how do we expect new-paradigm thinking to emerge if it does not come with a renaissance of religious experience?

DAVID: It must come with a renaissance of religious experience, and it does come today with a new explicit appreciation of religious experience. The sense of a deep inner communion with God was thought not long ago to be the privilege of "mystics." Today this sense of inner communion is widespread. Today we recognize that every human being can be a mystic of sorts. Of course, we should not forget that countless Christians throughout the ages were living in the strength of the divine life at the core of their being. Thus they were truly mystics. People like Meister Eckhart or Jakob Böhme or Julian of Norwich or John of the Cross, people whom we label mystics, were often those who gained notoriety by getting in trouble with the establishment. Countless others were nourished by sources of mystical life within their hearts and may have never even reflected on it. What keeps faith alive is always experiential knowledge of God's spirit within us.

FRITJOF: You see, in science, no matter what paradigm they function in, all agree that the basis of scientific knowledge is systematic observation.

DAVID: I think what happened progressively in the Christian tradition is that theology until recently separated itself from the very life of the Church and became desiccated, at least in some of its better-known representatives. Today this is no longer possible. Issues of new scientific discoveries, of political abuses or sexual equality or religious pluralism, and so on have a strong impact on theology. Unless theology addresses these issues, it runs the risk of becoming irrelevant.

THOMAS: There again, you see, to do justice to the history of it, you ought to name some of the best examples. For instance, Thomas Aquinas himself was without question a great mystic, a man of profound spiritual experience, but he lived his mystical life on a plane worlds distant from his theology. At the end of his life, when the tension between his experience and his theology had become intolerable, he said of his theological work, "It is all straw!"

DAVID: Thomas, earlier you mentioned four paradigms in Christian theology. Could you quickly run through those?

THOMAS: I'll try my best to be brief. A good outline is found in a book-length article on theology and its method by Cyprian Vagaggini, an Italian theologian who belongs to the Camaldolese Benedictine community in Italy.

DAVID: Yes, Cyprian Vagaggini is one who for hundreds, or maybe for thousands, of students was a great teacher all his life. He has really promoted a paradigm shift in theology. He's one of the key persons in the context of our conversation.

THOMAS: Vagaggini starts by looking at the history of Western thought in general. He underlines the anomalous character of Aristotle in relation to the other great philosophers. Aristotle, says Vagaggini, interrupts the general thrust of classical thought, which tended to unify the classical quest for wisdom around a total humanism and a total concern for human development—the human potential, we would say today. A key element in the development of Christian theology has been how much Aristotle has been brought into it.

At the beginning of Christianity, the New Testament already contains a theology, but one that is not systematic and not, properly speaking, dogmatic. Following the New Testament, four major theological paradigms emerge: the early or Patristic, the medieval Scholastic, the Positive-Scholastic, and finally the twentieth-century paradigm, which we are calling new-paradigm theology. The first great theological synthesis, the Patristic paradigm, begins to emerge in the third, fourth, and fifth centuries. This is what Vagaggini calls the Gnosis-Wisdom model, a theology whose purpose is to lead believers to a *gnosis* that is not abstract knowledge but a vision of reality that transforms the whole person.

FRITJOF: What about the Pauline interpretation?

THOMAS: Saint Paul is, without question, the first Christian theologian, but his theology does not have an overarching, systematic character. However, Paul's concern for the personal destiny of the believer, his centering of Christian life around the cross of Jesus, and above all his doctrine of salvation by grace through faith have become the great themes of theology ever since.

DAVID: And how about Origen?

THOMAS: Origen is also one of the great pioneers in theology. He set up the loom on which the Patristic synthesis was woven, because he basically invented the theological method. You might say that his great contribution was not so much the content of his thought as it was his method, a certain way of reading Scripture, a way of reading the Bible on many different levels. Origen is a central figure in the first great theological paradigm, the Gnosis-Wisdom model of the Patristic era.

The second paradigm is the great Scholastic systematization, with the input from the new Latin translations of Aristotle and the Islamic commentators on Aristotle.

FRITJOF: If you wanted to attach centuries?

THOMAS: You could date the Patristic era from the third century to about 1100. The Scholastic period then goes from the twelfth to the sixteenth century. Scholasticism is characterized by its strongly intellectual bias and its efforts to put faith into a coherent system with the aid of Aristotelian philosophical concepts, an attempt to make Aristotelian sense of Christian faith.

With the Reformation and the Catholic Counter-Reformation, you find the development of what is called Positive-Scholastic theology, which is a way of doing theology based on proof texts. You take passages from the Bible and passages from the early Fathers of the Church and passages from the *Summa* of Saint Thomas; then you use a syllogistic method in order to demonstrate that this, that, or the other article of dogmatic teaching is true and irrefutable.

DAVID: Maybe in this third period of theology, we have a parallel to a time in science, before experimental science was reintroduced in the Renaissance, in which science really consisted in reiterating what had been said a thousand years earlier by the Greek scientists. Those premodern scientists were repeating authoritative statements; they were not experimenting. Yet in their daily lives they were probably noticing phenomena that contradicted their theories; they just didn't systematically investigate them.

THOMAS: The Positive-Scholastic theology is characterized by its polemical and apologetical character. In other words, its aim is to defend Catholicism against the Protestants, then against the Enlightenment, and now against secularism, against Marxism, against all forms of modernism.

FRITJOF: Wouldn't you say that is still going on, that it reaches to the present?

THOMAS: Certainly it reaches to the present, but what we are in right now is, you might say, one of these chaotic intervals. Throughout the early twentieth century, Catholic theologians were trying to develop a new synthesis that would unite the intellectual approach to faith and religion with the experiential, while introducing also a strongly anthropological or humanistic element.

New-paradigm thinkers in contemporary theology

FRITJOF: That brings me to my next question. When we talk about new-paradigm thinking in theology, who are the representatives and who is the community sharing this new paradigm? Who would be theologians thinking in those ways? Are there a dozen, or are there a couple of hundred? How many are there?

DAVID: Of course, I can't give you an up-to-date count, but I can say with confidence that it's the majority. I don't even want to name those theologians who quickly come to mind as trailblazers for new-paradigm thinking. The decisive point is that most contemporary theologians are operating more or less within the new paradigm.

FRITJOF: This is certainly new to me, that there is a large community of theologians pursuing new thinking in theology.

DAVID: Yes. And that's all the more remarkable when you consider how many scientists today are still closed to new-paradigm thinking. But to make sure that I'm not overly optimistic, I would like to get Thomas's feedback on this point. Any naming of numbers would of course be ridiculous. Yet in the theological community worldwide someone who is not at least moving in the direction of what we are here calling the new paradigm would be looked at as outmoded and reactionary, not worth taking seriously, even if a few ultraconservatives entrench themselves in positions of influence and power.

THOMAS: This is because the search for a new theological paradigm is already a hundred years old. Toward the middle of the nineteenth century, some Catholic thinkers began to be aware of the need for a new approach in theology: John Henry Newman returned to the sources of an earlier theological paradigm, that of the Patristic era, and drew from them his ideas on the development of Christian doctrine and on the difference between notional (merely intellectual) assent and real assent in the act of faith. The German theologian Johann Moehler pursued much the same course, emphasizing the nonconceptual dimension of faith and the reality of the Church as a sacramental mystery and not just an institution, a "perfect society," as it was called then. In the course of this century, the urgent need for theological renewal became apparent to a great number of Catholics, even outside the academic community. Finally, the Second Vatican Council (1962–66) put an official seal of approval on the search for a new theological paradigm and provided a common ground for the new paradigm, which virtually everyone accepted from then on.

DAVID: Right. In other words, theologians were pushing for a paradigm shift, and what kept it back for a fairly long time was the Church establishment. By the way, is there anything comparable in the scientific world to the establishment of the Church that would hold back a paradigm shift?

FRITJOF: Of course. It would be the scientific establishment, including the grant-giving bodies. Today in the life sciences, for example, there are two major directions. One is molecular biology, genetic engineering and all that. The other one is ecology. I would say culturally and socially, ecology is far more important, but it hardly gets any money, whereas everything is poured into molecular biology. And the new thinking definitely is in systems biology (neural networks, self-organization, autopoiesis, etc.), which is closely related to ecology.

DAVID: How interesting! This is an area in which we didn't at all expect parallels; yet there's a most striking parallel between science and theology.

FRITJOF: So in science I think it's money, grants, the academic institutions. And in the Church, I guess, it's another kind of power, not financial power.

DAVID: Yes, the power to forbid theologians to speak, the power to bar them from positions where they will be heard. Hans Küng continues to teach, but he's not allowed to call himself a Catholic theologian. He now teaches at an institute for world religions, not the Catholic theology faculty. But this has made him all the more aware of a need for relating Christian theology to other religions and to science and to literature, very much in the spirit of the Second Vatican Council.

FRITJOF: So you seem to have the funny situation that Vatican II encouraged a lot of things that the establishment now does not want. Right?

THOMAS: There are still persons in the Church who do not fully accept Vatican II, and there are those who would even turn back the clock if they could, which is of course impossible. Part of what created the climate favorable to change in the Church was the experience of the unsuccessful attempt to silence some of the best Catholic thinkers from the 1930s to the 1960s: for example, Henri de Lubac and Yves Congar, two great French theologians. On the frontier between theology and the natural sciences, the Jesuit paleontologist Pierre Teilhard de Chardin posed a challenge to old-paradigm thinking in both camps; he was forbidden to publish any of his theological or philosophical writings during his lifetime. But by the time of the Second Vatican Council, it became apparent that a new theological orientation was needed for the ongoing dialogue of the Church with contemporary culture, perhaps even for the survival of Christianity.

DAVID: The shift was prompted not only by individual theologians but also by that profound groundswell of which you spoke, Thomas. All this finally led to the changes that surfaced in Vatican II. The initiative came largely out of German and French Benedictine monasteries.

FRITJOF: The groundswell would be comparable to the anomalies in the scientific paradigm, because the groundswell said, "This is not compatible with my religious experience or with my experience in life."

DAVID: And of course it came not only out of the monasteries. But a decisive contribution was made by monasteries, precisely because they are laboratories for religious experience.

THOMAS: Now that we're talking about monasteries, let me mention the name of a very simple, ordinary monk who, at the start of this century, made an enormous contribution to the paradigm shift in Catholic theology—Lambert Baudouin. He was a Belgian Benedictine who founded, almost single-handedly, both the liturgical movement in the Catholic Church and the ecumenical movement, especially the dialogue with the Eastern Orthodox Church but also with the Anglican communion and with Protestants. Baudouin proposed a return to an experiential and celebrative theology, as a preparation for the acting-out of the mystery in ritual; his liturgical theology was a reflection on the faith open even to outsiders, near and far. So theology today has come to be sacramental, mystery oriented, and ecumenical.

Father Lambert was imprisoned in a monastery and silenced by the Church, but he lived just long enough to see Pope John XXIII call for a new council of the Church, which would finally do justice to his ideas.

FRITJOF: What were those ideas?

THOMAS: For one thing, Baudouin realized that the great mass of Europeans were simply turned off by Christianity. Many clung to Christianity and continued to attend church, not because it gave meaning to their own lives and their personal spiritual experience but because there was no alternative. The only alternative was complete secularism, which is obviously not a spiritual alternative. So they clung to the forms, but the forms were not nourishing them. Baudouin saw that a valid response to the spiritual needs of alienated Christians had to be based on a theology and a pastoral practice that were both ecumenical and centered on the celebration of the Christ-mystery in liturgy.

4 The Christian Paradigm

FRITJOF: Within the context that we have established so far—religious experience, intellectual reflection on it, celebration of the experience, and behavior that goes with it, which leads to morals—within that context, which, I presume, holds for all religions, what is typically Christian?

THOMAS: I find it very difficult to articulate what is specifically Christian in a way that excludes the religious experience that emerges in other religions. It's hard for me to say whether any authentic religious experience can be excluded from my concept of Christianity, catholic Christianity, perhaps with a small *c* if you wish.

FRITJOF: But my question does not just concern religious experience. It concerns all the other aspects as well, the intellectual reflection, the interpretation, the analysis, the rituals, the morals. What, in all of that, is typically Christian?

The historic personage of Jesus Christ

THOMAS: What is specific to Christianity is the person of Jesus and the event of his life, death, and resurrection. And then the radiation of this historical person through the community of those who believe in him and who try to live as he did, a life of self-sacrificing love.

In my own personal experience, I find that the very nature of this mystery of Jesus is such that it cannot be monopolized by the Church. In fact many Hindus, Buddhists, and others are now seeking to understand Jesus in terms of their own traditions; some have arrived at a deep understanding of him. I consider this highly significant from a theological viewpoint. The mystery of Jesus is specific to Christianity, but it cannot be monopolized by Christian believers, because it is universal.

DAVID: I would say, if you ask me what is specifically Christian, let's not stop at the Churches. When can you call something Christian? When it has a decisive relationship to Jesus Christ, to that historic personage of Jesus Christ. There are many, many degrees of closeness of relationship, but as long as it is a decisive relationship, I would call it Christian. In other words, I would agree with Thomas that there are Christian elements nowadays in Buddhism, there are Christian elements in contemporary Hinduism.

FRITJOF: Now what makes Christianity itself Christian?

DAVID: Well, the decisive thing is the religious experience of Jesus himself. It all goes back to that particular human being, and I cannot see any other way of understanding Jesus than that he was a mystic. For me mysticism—in a very broad definition, which is quite generally accepted —is the experience of communion with Ultimate Reality. Jesus had a particularly intimate, in some respect new experience of communion with Ultimate Reality. He did not hesitate to relate to God with an unheard-of intimacy. By his life and by his teaching, Jesus communicated to many others this mystic closeness to God.

The Kingdom of God

DAVID: Jesus put the social implications of mystic awareness in terms of the Kingdom of God. That's the key word in the message of Jesus.

His followers took the next step; theirs was a teaching *about* Jesus. But we must always refer back to the teaching *of* Jesus himself. Jesus had a deep mystic experience of God and spoke about it, lived it, in terms of the Kingdom of God. "Kingdom of God" meant for Jesus "the saving power of God made manifest in human history." For Jews at the time of Jesus, salvation was a matter of the community to which they belonged. For us this communal aspect of salvation is almost impossible to appreciate except in terms of global community. Because we are so individualistic, we have to translate what God's saving power made manifest means to us today.

For us God's saving power is manifest in the religious experience, the experience of limitless belonging. In our peak moments we experience "saving" power rescuing us, bringing us out of that which is most foreign to this sense of belonging, namely, alienation. The experience that we belong is the basis for Jesus' preaching of the Kingdom, expressed in our contemporary terms. Then, the primary reference was to the community of the chosen people. But for us it is more broadly the experience of belonging and its social consequences.

The preaching of Jesus stands or falls on that. He preached as much by how he lived as by what he said. And that's what he lived—that mystic sense of limitless belonging and its translation into a radically new kind of society.

Christian love

FRITJOF: How is Christian love related to that?

DAVID: Love is saying yes to belonging. That's my definition of love, pure and simple. Anything that we call love, as far as I can see, is in some way related to this yes. What ties all the various notions of love together, from sexual love to love of your pets to love of your country and love of the world and love of the environment, what ties them all together is that in each of those cases we are saying yes to belonging. And that saying yes is not just an intellectual assent; it has profound moral implications. It means, as I have said before, acting the way people act when they belong together.

FRITJOF: This would not be romantic love, falling in love.

DAVID: No, it's rather a rising in love than a falling in love, although romantic love, too, shows you how blissful it is to belong and to act accordingly. Romantic love is a good example of a joyful yes! That is why we jump quickly to romantic love as an illustration of love in general, because there we experience how wonderful it is to belong and to act accordingly.

THOMAS: It's the primary metaphor of love also for the Bible, for example, in the Song of Songs. It's also the primary metaphor in Tantric Hinduism: the union of Shiva and Shakti.

FRITJOF: So when you spoke about the religious experience earlier, this was already a specifically Christian way of speaking about it.

DAVID: Yes, it was, because for us the peak experiences, or religious experiences or mystic experiences—and all of these are just different terms for one and the same basic reality—could also be called, in specific Christian terms, Kingdom moments. This is today our only access to that strange term Kingdom. We speak of the animal kingdom and of the plant kingdom and so forth. And so the Kingdom of God is our belonging to this great cosmic reality.

FRITJOF: Over the last ten years, I have come to see spirituality, or what you would call religious experience, as the mode of consciousness where we feel connected to the cosmos as a whole. That is very close to what you're saying. But there is a difference between being connected and belonging. Belonging has, to me at least, an affective coloring. It's slightly different.

Conversion

DAVID: Yes, and this is the point where we have to push this Jesus paradigm a little further. The message of Jesus goes further than the Kingdom. There is a second half that inseparably belongs to the Kingdom, and that is conversion. Conversion means "living accordingly." Therefore, you have from the very beginning a strong moral thrust to Christianity, stronger, I think, than in other religions. That might be one of the distinguishing marks. But it is not moralistic. Conversion means something quite different from what is often presented popularly as such. It is not the repentance by which you make up for your sins so that God will accept you. It is the exact opposite: Conversion springs from the conviction, already implied in the religious experience, *that you have been accepted.* And now live accordingly! That is the preaching of Jesus. It is summed up in the double statement of Paul: "By grace—gratis, gratuitously—you have been saved," and "Live worthy of that calling." Kingdom and conversion are two sides of one coin.

THOMAS: Let me emphasize the words "by grace you have been saved." The moral dimension of Christianity is always consequent on an inner transformation experienced as a free gift; it's not simply a matter of willpower, of deciding to give up my bad habits and to adopt other habits. Rather it is divinization from within, a datum of experience that Christians understand as an action of God within the person.

Jesus and Buddha

FRITJOF: I was just going to say something very similar in connection with Buddhism. It seems to me that what you just said is that, by grace or by revelation, you belong to the cosmos, to that great unity. And then as a consequence of this belonging, you live accordingly. The way I understand Buddhism is that the way to spiritual experience or enlightenment is a moral life. You have to live right. The Buddha says, "You live according to the Eightfold Path," which is right livelihood, right thinking, right speaking, and so on. Then, if you live right, you will be able to detach yourself from the fleeting moments, from the fact that everything dies and is in transition. And then you will have a spiritual insight.

DAVID: Do you see in this a contradiction to the message of Jesus?

FRITJOF: Yes, the sequence is opposite.

DAVID: I don't think so. And I base this contention not on my Christian point of view but on my understanding of Buddhism. Of course, I may be wrong in my understanding, but this is how I see it: I would agree with the sequence you presented, but I would suggest that the end is also the beginning. Precisely because cosmic harmony is a given, you *find* your real self by attuning yourself to this harmony.

FRITJOF: Actually this is true, because they say you don't meditate to achieve Buddhahood. You meditate because you are a Buddha.

DAVID: See how close the parallel is with Jesus' teaching? On the deepest level there is no difference. There is, however, an enormous historic distinction. The whole setting in which Buddha formally proclaimed this insight and the setting in which Jesus insinuated it are so different. But even then, there are some historical parallels. In Judaism the situation out of which Jesus breaks is not dissimilar to the situation in Hinduism out of which Buddha breaks.

THOMAS: The situation that Jesus faced was in some ways similar to the historical situation that the Buddha emerged from or had to face—the problem of religious formalism and of the manipulation of the common people's religious needs on the part of a dominant sacerdotal caste. Like Buddha, Jesus came "not to destroy but to fulfill" and to proclaim that the way to illumination and liberation was open for every human person. The Buddha understood illumination as the "realization" of that which eternally *is*. Likewise, in the words of Saint Paul, the Christian paradox is "Become what you are! You have risen together with Christ, you have ascended into heaven with Christ, you have been enthroned with him." To express that which we are in the mind of God, Saint Paul uses a whole series of verbs with the prefix *syn* in Greek, which means "with, together with"—*con* in Latin. All of this has taken place; therefore you must live your life accordingly and, in other words, become what you are. The becoming is a consequence of being. Grace is also the givenness of nature. Even the division . . . there is no division.

DAVID: But I think there is an important difference between the history of Jesus and the history of Buddha. With Jesus this idea of the Kingdom leads to dramatic social implications. Because of that intimacy with God, as children of the Father, we also are brothers and sisters among one another. And so Jesus goes around as the one who builds everybody up and builds community. The authoritarian authorities lord it over everybody.

"But with you, it must be different," Jesus says. "The greatest among you must be the servant of all." That is really at the core of his message. And that has made of Christianity a leaven in society ever since, a yeast for radical changes. That is also the reason why Jesus is put to death. He is subversive to the religious establishment, because he builds up people's inner authority, while authoritarianism puts them down. To the political establishment he is equally dangerous, and for the same reason. That new understanding of authority is at the heart of the Christian message. It goes back to Jesus, to the very starting point of Christianity.

Later, after his death and resurrection, you get the Christianity *about* Jesus rather than the Christianity *of* Jesus. I do not think that there is a contradiction between the two, but there certainly is a different viewpoint. While Jesus was preaching the Kingdom of God, the Church ever since the beginning is preaching Jesus. That's fine, as long as we don't allow a private devotion to Jesus to replace the radical social challenge of God's Kingdom.

The Trinity

FRITJOF: I was not expecting that this would lead us so much to talk about the person of Jesus Christ, but since we are there, let me ask you both about his God-nature and resurrection. Whenever you speak about these things, I have a lot of baggage from the past that bothers me. You say that Jesus was a mystic who had a very intimate relationship with the Ultimate Reality that you experience in the mystical or religious experience, and therefore he called himself the Son of God.

DAVID: He didn't call himself that. It is historically well established that the "Son of God" teaching is *about* Jesus Christ. He himself simply *acted* as one intimately connected with God, and so he empowered others to live that way.

FRITJOF: He talked about the "Father and I," right?

THOMAS: One thing that we do know about the relationship of Jesus to God is that when he prayed, he gave God a name that is not found on the lips of any of his contemporaries: He called God Abba, which is the least patriarchal masculine image that can be attributed to God. The least patriarchal, because it means, in good English, "Daddy." That was his prayer, "Abba, Daddy!"

DAVID: We also know historically that he gave to women a position totally different from the one they held in society at that time.

FRITJOF: Let me ask you about the God-nature of Jesus. If he says "I am God," in the sense of the mystic, of the "That art Thou," then he is completely aligned with all mystics. But this is not the teaching of the Church. When you talk about the Trinity, he has a special position. God appears in three forms.

DAVID: Let me speak from my own understanding. You say that Jesus has this mystic intimacy with the divine, and therefore he's perfectly in line with the mystics. I, as a believing Christian who accepts the dogmas of the Church, can still say yes, this is so. This does not contradict trinitarian theology, because none of the statements that theology makes about Jesus must be allowed to separate Jesus from us. What separates Jesus from us is not the Christian dogma but a widespread misunderstanding of Christian dogma. This misunderstanding springs from our individualism—an "ism"—which is incompatible with the teaching of Jesus, with the outlook of the Bible, and with the correct understanding of Christian dogma. So in other words, yes, we can affirm all these trinitarian teachings about Jesus, even that he is the second person of the Trinity.

FRITJOF: But how do you affirm them?

DAVID: You affirm that the Trinity includes you and me! Because you're not allowed to speak about Jesus as being separate from you.

FRITJOF: So what's the Trinity then? I don't understand this at all. What is the trinitarian God?

THOMAS: The reason the doctrine of the Trinity was formulated, I am convinced, the ultimate reason, was in order to guarantee the total divinization of every single human being. This is what we call the soteriological argument, the ultimate argument of Saint Athanasius, who was the great defender of the Council of Nicaea, the first general council of the Church, in the fourth century. To put it simply, if Jesus is not the Second Person of the Trinity, then you and I are not sharers in the divine nature. "God became human in order that every human being may become God": this axiom is repeated by Athanasius and a whole series of early Christian teachers. The theme of divinization is present in the minds of all the original formulators of this dogma.

FRITJOF: Other traditions also have this theme of divinization. In Hinduism, for example, the human individual (Atman) and the divine reality (Brahman) are said to be one and the same, "That art Thou." In those traditions, however, there seem to be only two entities, the self and the divine, whereas in Christianity there are three. Why the Trinity? Why the Holy Spirit?

DAVID: You have it also in Hinduism. From a Christian point of view, the Holy Spirit is there when the Hindu says, "Atman is Brahman." No one can say—I am paraphrasing Saint Paul—Atman is Brahman except in the Holy Spirit. No one can know the divine reality except by means of God's own self-knowledge. We actually share God's self-knowledge in and through the Holy Spirit. Saint Paul has a tremendous passage in his first letter to the Corinthians: no human person knows what is in the mind of another human person. Our deepest knowledge of ourselves is only available to our own spirit, as he says. Only your spirit knows your inner depth, and only my spirit knows my depths. Likewise, no one knows the depths of the divine reality except the spirit of God. Now, you might think that the conclusion of these two premises would be that therefore no human being can possibly know God; if we can't even know another human being deep down, how can we know God? But Paul makes an incredible leap and says, "We have received the spirit of God, so that we may know the gifts of God." In other words, we know God from within; we share in God's own self-knowledge. If we understand it thus, the Trinity is a way of speaking about our human relatedness to the divine reality. It is a teaching rooted in our mystic experience: God is knower, known, and knowing.

The resurrection

FRITJOF: Okay, now you have allayed my bad memories or my fear in that respect. Now what about the resurrection? You said very nonchalantly a while ago, "after his death and resurrection." In the Catholicism that I learned in school, the resurrection was taken as proof that Jesus is God. He rose from the dead.

THOMAS: That's not theology. That is apologetics. The resurrection of Jesus as a "proof" of his divinity is old-paradigm theology, and no responsible theologian is going to dredge that up today.

New-paradigm thinking would put it this way, very roughly: The experience that Jesus had of being raised from the dead is an incommunicable experience; it belongs to him alone. What his disciples experienced was Jesus present to them in a new way, different from his physical presence before death, but no less real. Seeing the risen Jesus, the disciples realized that they also had risen and would rise from the dead with him and in him. In other words, they experienced Jesus as "the firstborn from the dead," the beginning and cause of a new, resurrected humanity. And so we have the great argument of Saint Paul, who said, "How can you talk about Jesus as risen, if we don't *all* rise from the dead?"

FRITJOF: So it's the same thing really as being God.

THOMAS: It's parallel to that. The important thing is that the earliest expressions of Christian faith were centered on the event that followed the death of Jesus on the cross and that is the key to understanding his death as God's saving power made manifest. The reality of a great teacher, of a wonderful, lovable person, being subjected to capital punishment on the basis of ambiguous accusations can not possibly, for any intelligent human being, be a manifestation of the saving power of God. It's a manifestation of human violence and brutality, of ignorance, not the manifestation of the saving power of God. But it becomes this, through an experience that is unaccountable, that is basically indefinable, certainly mystical: the disciples' experience of Jesus as the Risen One.

DAVID: How would you feel if I put it this way: First of all, there is no point in speaking about the death and resurrection of Jesus, as is unfortunately often done, without speaking about his life.

THOMAS: Well, you see, the crucifixion simply ends a beautiful life. But it doesn't communicate this beautiful life. The experience of seeing and touching the risen Jesus convinced his disciples that this beautiful life was not something that they could only remember; it was also something that became part of them, that they themselves could live. In other words, the Kingdom becomes Jesus through the resurrection.

DAVID: That's why the life of Jesus is so important. In the way Jesus lives he takes an antiauthoritarian stance in the world, and that stance grows out of his mystic intimacy with God. Looking at Jesus, we see how one lives when one has this mystic intimacy with God, when one says yes to limitless belonging. That's what he lives. If one lives this way in the kind of world we have created, one will be squelched or in one way or the other crucified. Now the question arises, Is that the end? The teaching of the resurrection is the affirmation that it's not the end. This kind of aliveness cannot be extinguished. He died, he really died, and behold, he lives!

Where does he live? Let's not make the mistake of saying he is here or there. No. A rarely cited early Christian answer is this: "His life is hidden in God." Paul doesn't say it in these words; he says, "*Our* life is hidden *with Christ* in God." But that implies that Christ's life is hidden in God. God's presence in this world is hidden, and yet it is the most tangible thing for anybody who lives with full awareness. God's presence is everywhere; still, it is a hidden presence. Jesus died, and yet he is alive, and his life is hidden in God. He is also alive in us. There is no way of pointing a finger and saying, "Look!" or "Zap! He came out from the tomb." Resurrection is not revivification; it is not survival; it is not a matter of saying, "There he is!" It's a hidden reality, but it is a reality, and we can live in the strength of its power. And that is all we need to know about the resurrection.

III

The Current Shift of Paradigms (General Comments)

FRITJOF: I would like to add some general comments and questions about the paradigm shift in science and theology. As far as the old paradigm is concerned, I think it has two main roots. One is mechanistic science, the science of the seventeenth century developed by Galileo, Descartes, Newton, Bacon, and their contemporaries. The other is the patriarchal value system which, of course, derives from much older patriarchal attitudes, behavior patterns, beliefs. And the two are very closely intertwined.

The new paradigm may be called holistic, emphasizing the whole more than the parts, or it may be called ecological, and that's actually the term I prefer.

Holism and ecology

FRITJOF: In fact, I've recently emphasized that it's important to know the difference between holistic and ecological. An ecological worldview is holistic, but it's more than that. It looks not only at something as a whole but also at how this whole is embedded into larger wholes. This is especially important when you study living systems—living organisms, ecosystems, and so on—but it can be applied also to nonliving things. The ecological view of a bicycle, for example, would imply seeing it as a whole—the functional interrelatedness of all its parts—and also asking, Where does the rubber for the tires come from? Where does the metal come from? What is the effect on the environment of riding a bicycle? And so on. It embeds the whole into larger wholes.

That is a very important difference, and because this is so important to the new paradigm, I prefer to call it ecological.

Ecology and religion

FRITJOF: The term *ecological* has another aspect that is extremely relevant to us here. Ecological awareness and ecological consciousness goes far beyond science, and at the deepest level it joins with religious awareness and religious experience. Because at the deepest level, ecological awareness is an awareness of the fundamental interconnectedness and interdependence of all phenomena and of this embeddedness in the cosmos. And, of course, the notions of being embedded in the cosmos, and of belonging to the cosmos, are very similar. This is where ecology and religion meet. And this is also why the new-paradigm thinking in science has these surprising parallels to thinking in spiritual traditions; for example, the parallels to Eastern mysticism, which I explored in *The Tao of Physics*. The worldview now emerging from modern science is an ecological view, and ecological awareness at its deepest level is spiritual or religious awareness. And this is why the new paradigm, within science and even more outside it, is accompanied by a new rise of spirituality, particularly a new kind of earth-centered spirituality.

Ecological and ecumenical

DAVID: We see eye to eye on that one. I want to point out another interesting parallel. Where you say, "ecological," we say, "ecumenical." That is not only a play on words; it is the deeper truth that in both cases we have the intuition of an earth household, because the root of both terms is the Greek word *oikos,* "house."

FRITJOF: What are the implications?

THOMAS: Well, *oikos* refers to the inhabited world, the house of humanity.

DAVID: To the "Earth Household," as Gary Snyder calls it.

FRITJOF: Only to the human realm?

DAVID: No, no. We want to stress a wider belonging, not restricted to humans.

FRITJOF: What is the difference, then, between ecological and ecumenical? Is it a purely conventional difference, that one is used by theologians and the other by scientists?

THOMAS: There is a difference, and it is more than conventional. The concern in "ecological," as I understand it, is the sense of belonging to the greater whole of the physical universe, of the Earth, as a whole living system. Whereas "ecumenical" focuses on our belonging to a global culture. I think, perhaps, there's a certain "anthropocentrism" on the theological side, but not in the sense of "man's" dominance over nature. The theologian's concern is to arrive at the highest common bond of humanity on many different levels: the vital level of simply living and belonging to the universe, but also on the level of culture, where there are universal values, expressed in an enormous variety of ways but common to all humanity.

FRITJOF: This is an important point. Ecologists often have a tendency to be biologistic, in the sense that they have a tendency to neglect culture, because ecosystems don't have culture. Culture is a human phenomenon. Ecologists tend to neglect the cultural dimension of the Earth Household. So it's very good to say that "ecumenical" focuses on that. Maybe it tends to neglect the other side, the biological. Certainly both are needed.

DAVID: As often as possible, I try to use the term Earth Household. It's such a good expression. Ecumenical and ecological are sort of abstract, sitting out there; but the moment you say Earth Household, there you have it. Do you know the short poem by D. H. Lawrence called "Pax"? It's significant that he should have called it "Pax," because the Pax Benedictina of the Middle Ages held the world together as an Earth Household, at least the way it was understood then. This is how the poem goes:

Pax

All that matters is to be at one with the living God
to be a creature in the house of the God of Life.

Like a cat asleep on a chair
at peace, in peace
and at one with the master of the house, with the mistress,
at home, at home in the house of the living,
sleeping on the hearth, and yawning before the fire.

Sleeping on the hearth of the living world,
yawning at home before the fire of life
feeling the presence of the living God
like a great reassurance
a deep calm in the heart
a presence
as of a master sitting at the board
in his own and greater being,
in the house of life.

FRITJOF: That's beautiful.

DAVID: It's all intuition, there's not much left brain in it. But what matters is all there.

THOMAS: Theology is there, too. Poetry is an entirely appropriate medium of theological discourse.

Systems theory

THOMAS: I don't know where to put this, it's so elementary, but the term sometimes drifts out of clarity for me, the term *systems theory*. What exactly is systems theory?

FRITJOF: I'm very glad you asked that, because I left that out. I said I wanted to call the new paradigm an ecological paradigm. And to me systems theory is the scientific formulation of the ecological worldview.

Let me give you a very brief historical sketch. One important root of systems theory lies in cybernetics. The 1940s saw the creation of cybernetics. Another root is more of a systems philosophy. Ludwig von Bertalanffy was the great figure in that development. Out of cybernetics came two schools of thought, both of which are systems theories. One is the school associated with John von Neumann, who was a mathematical genius, the inventor of the computer, author of a very important book on quantum mechanics and of many other writings. This school of thought is still mechanistic systems theory; it's a very sophisticated mechanism, but it deals with input-output systems, and it created the model of living organisms as information-processing machines.

The other school is associated with Norbert Wiener, and it starts from the concept of self-organization. It sees living systems as self-organizing. In the 1940s and 1950s and in the decades that followed, the John von Neumann school was predominant with the whole success of cybernetics, the development of computers, these input-output systems, and the like. The self-organizing school of thought had a hiatus and went to sleep until it was revived at the beginning of the 1960s. And this is now the most exciting school of thought when it comes to living systems. Self-organization, in other words, autonomy, is seen as the hallmark of life, and this notion is explored in a variety of contexts, at the level of cells (Humberto Maturana, Francisco Varela), at the level of family (the Milan school of family therapy), and at the level of society (Niklas Luhmann).

DAVID: We know that living systems are embedded in other, larger, living systems. What would you call the largest system? How would you speak about it?

FRITJOF: As far as science today is concerned, and as far as a definition of life is concerned, the largest living system is the Earth. That is the Gaia Hypothesis, that the Earth is a living system. The solar system is not thought of as a living system by most people. And then when it goes beyond the solar system to the galaxy and the universe as a whole, you leave the life sciences, except for some very controversial speculations. So I would say the largest living system that scientists agree upon is the planet.

New thinking and new values

FRITJOF: I also would like to show you a striking and somewhat surprising pattern of the paradigm change, a connection between thinking and values. It turns out that the old thinking and the old values hang together, are very closely intertwined. And correspondingly the new thinking and the new values are closely intertwined.

In both cases, thinking and values, there is a shift of emphasis from self-assertion to integration. That's the best way I've found to characterize those groups of modes of thinking and of values.

In thinking, the shift has been from the rational to the intuitive. Rational thinking consists in compartmentalizing, distinguishing, categorizing. That's very much connected with the whole notion of the self as a distinct category, so it's clearly self-assertive. Analysis is this method of distinguishing and categorizing, and there has been a shift from analysis to synthesis; a shift from reductionism to holism, from linear thinking to nonlinear thinking.

As far as values are concerned, you have a shift from competition to cooperation—very clearly a shift from self-assertion to integration; from expansion to conservation; from quantity to quality; from domination to partnership (as Riane Eisler has emphasized).

Now, if you look at this from the systems point of view, from the point of view of living systems, you realize that since all living systems are embedded in larger systems, they have this dual nature that Arthur Koestler called a Janus nature. On the one hand, a living system is an integrated whole with its own individuality, and it has the tendency to assert itself and to preserve that individuality. As part of the larger whole, it needs to integrate itself into that larger whole. It's very important to realize that those are opposite and contradictory tendencies. We need a dynamic balance between them, and that's essential for physical and mental health. The Chinese picked this up with great intuitive power. In order to have a healthy life, you need to assert yourself and you need to integrate yourself.

I think culturally and socially you can say that the pendulum has swung between those two tendencies. For instance, the Middle Ages were characterized by a lot of integration but also by a lack of self-assertion.

DAVID: Overemphasis on integration.

FRITJOF: But then with the Renaissance, you have the emergence of individuality. Then it went further in the nineteenth century, and later, especially here in America, you have an overemphasis on individuality —the cowboy ethic, rugged individualism, and so on.

The emergence of individuality gave rise to individualism all over the Western world, but you had socialism as a countertendency. This then went too far in the socialist countries, which are now looking for a balance. Humanism, of course, is the key word for the emergence of individuality. And so Gorbachev and several Marxist philosophers before him have been talking about a "new humanism." In Prague in 1968, Dubcek introduced a "socialism with a human face." Similarly, E. F. Schumacher was talking about technology with a human face, because technology had become so oppressive.

I have taken this interplay between these tendencies, self-assertion and integration, as my framework to talk about values in contemporary society, where you can see consistently an overemphasis of self-assertion and neglect of integration.

The other important connection is to the patriarchal value system, because the self-assertive values and modes of thinking are the masculine ones. Whether this is biological or cultural is a very tricky question, and I don't want to go into this. But in most cultures, and certainly in our culture, the self-assertive ways of thinking and the self-assertive values have been associated with men, with manliness, and have been given political power.

THOMAS: Would you say that, as ways of knowing, the theories associated with self-assertion give different results from those associated with integration? In other words, you arrive at a different content of knowledge, depending upon which mode of thinking you use. If you use the rational-analytic-reductionist-linear mode, you're going to learn certain things about nature but not others. Whereas if you use the intuitive-synthetic-holistic-nonlinear mode, you'll learn other things.

FRITJOF: Yes, but you also have to realize that you cannot use just one. In science you always need both.

DAVID: Is there not another term that one could use rather than rational to indicate the polar opposite of intuitive?

THOMAS: I think the nearest thing would be conceptual and nonconceptual kinds of knowledge. There's also an intuitive conceptualization, but concepts are most often formed through rational process, as the fruit of deductive reasoning.

DAVID: I'm very sensitive to a danger implicit in expressing it in this way; namely, that you equate intuitive with irrational, and that would be terribly wrong.

FRITJOF: Let me tell you what I mean without using any of these terms, and we'll come up with something. The self-assertive mode is a way of thinking that categorizes, that divides, that takes to pieces, that delineates. The other one is a way of perceiving nonlinear patterns, a synthesis of a nonlinear pattern. Intuition, to me, is an immediate perception of the whole, of a gestalt.

DAVID: The very word *intuition* means that you "look into" it. You take so deep a look that you see an inner coherence. But that's a perfectly rational way of dealing with the situation.

FRITJOF: No, I wouldn't call it rational, because I can't talk about it. To me rational is what you can talk about.

THOMAS: Then maybe you should call it not rational but discursive.

DAVID: . . . *discursive* and intuitive, that's a fine pair of opposite terms! Now I'm satisfied.
      Let's ask the question of ourselves: Is there a general shift in thinking and in values from self-assertion to integration also in theology? My intuitive response is Yes! Emphatically so. Let's see if some analysis will prove this intuition correct.

THOMAS: I think that, from a number of different viewpoints, this could be borne out in the contemporary theological discussion. For one thing, the apologetical and polemical thrust of most Positive-Scholastic theology tends to suggest the self-assertive mode. Whereas the ecumenical orientation of most contemporary or new-paradigm theology suggests the integrative. In other words, true fidelity to one's tradition requires a full and open understanding of other traditions.

DAVID: Also, more specifically, there is this switch from theological propositions to story telling. Originally all theological insights were stories before they became propositions. Why don't we turn them into stories again? Many ask this question today. That means a switch from the discursive to the intuitive, the story is intuitive; from the analytic to the synthetic, the story is synthetic; from the reductive to the holistic, because the story is a whole, greater than the sum total of its parts.

THOMAS: Of course, you wouldn't want to limit it to the narrative literary genre. You could also say that there is a shift from the propositional to the poetic or metaphorical.

DAVID: Yes, or from the abstract to the experiential. All this fits in.

FRITJOF: Story telling, by the way, was the preferred mode of Gregory Bateson, who was one of the key figures in the development of systems thinking. In his presentation Bateson was essentially a storyteller. His way of showing the connectedness of various patterns was through a story.

Mission

DAVID: Then, on the side of values, a fine example for the paradigm shift would be missionary activity, it seems to me. Missionary work used to be almost synonymous with competition, expansion, domination, of masculine emphasis on quantity—how many can we baptize in a hurry?

FRITJOF: And what is mission now?

DAVID: It went through an enormous crisis in recent decades. There are very few missionaries today who would try to turn the clock back. Basically *witness* is the key word today, not proselytizing.

THOMAS: Witness and dialogue. In other words, our presence among these people and their religions, especially in Asia, is a presence of dialogue.

FRITJOF: So the aim of mission is no longer to convert people to Catholicism?

THOMAS: No. In fact, it never was. The missionary's aim is to be a witness to the good news of God's universal plan of salvation. "Conversion" is not something the missionary does; it is uniquely an action of God within the heart of one who realizes, "This is good news *for me!*"

DAVID: There are now whole missionary groups who go into places where they know they will not make converts.

THOMAS: One religious order's mission explicitly excludes preaching, converting, baptizing, and that is the Missionaries of Charity of Mother Teresa. Her mission is exclusively the work of love. In other words, she wants her sisters to witness to their faith solely through prayer and the works of love.

FRITJOF: What does that mean: "to witness to their faith"?

THOMAS: To make known their faith not only by preaching it, but above all by living it. You see, the difference between witnessing and preaching, with the slight negative overtones that preaching can have, is that witnessing is not projected through my ego. In other words, I am simply present in order to let a great truth shine through me. In the end, I disappear, and the truth shines forth in those to whom I am present.

DAVID: Please know that this is not a surreptitious way of getting others to sign up as Christians. It is simply a witness to our common humanity. That witness is always needed. Today we are sensitive to the great mistakes missionaries have made in the past and to the great short-comings of Western colonialism that went hand in hand with mission. But we are apt to close our eyes to the serious shortcomings of many societies to whom the missionaries went. I admire the cultural integrity of those societies. But they were often in bondage to fear, in bondage to systems that kept their human potential suppressed. These are not things one often speaks about today, but, in all fairness, they deserve to be mentioned. In this context, mission means that you give witness to human dignity as Jesus did. Jesus wasn't proselytizing, he was liberat-ing. He gave witness to the dignity of every single human being in the particular setting of his time and place. To do this remains the task of Christian mission.

FRITJOF: Now for somebody like Mother Teresa or any of these mis-sionaries who do not preach and do not baptize, what is their purpose in witnessing in Asia or Africa? Why not do it right here?

DAVID: They do it right here, too. They do it everywhere.

FRITJOF: And they call themselves "missionaries" also here?

DAVID: Missionaries means simply "people who are sent." According to the Gospels, Jesus sends out his disciples because they are so full of enthusiasm for the new life he opens up for them. When you are enthusiastic about some good film that you have seen, you become a sort of missionary for Fellini or Ingmar Bergman among your friends and colleagues.

FRITJOF: So why would you be sent to Thailand as a Catholic missionary?

DAVID: You may be sent anyplace where there is oppression, exploitation, human misery. For example, members of a group called the Little Brothers of Jesus and the Little Sisters of Jesus live here in America and in many other parts of the world, in the slums, with the oppressed, the poor. They spread joy, but they have no permission to preach.

FRITJOF: So here the idea is not to go to Thailand because they have never heard of Christianity but to go to Thailand if there is a particular oppressive situation and to insert oneself into that situation.

THOMAS: To insert oneself as a bearer of the good news of God's Kingdom. How this is to be done, and how we are to relate mission to dialogue, still remain open questions in the Church at this stage in the paradigm shift.

What's new in the "new" paradigm?

DAVID: When we speak about the old paradigm in science or in theology, in both cases we are not talking about the oldest paradigm. The so-called new paradigm is really a recovery of our most ancient intuition.

FRITJOF: Yes, but it is more than that. The social paradigm change, the social and cultural change, is more than just a recovery. If you compare the emerging holistic worldview of today and the holistic worldview of the Middle Ages, you see many fascinating parallels. Then, the Cartesian paradigm, which we now call the old paradigm, emerged through the Renaissance and was formalized by Descartes and Newton and was in contradiction to much of the medieval paradigm. Now we are recovering some of the aspects of the medieval paradigm and older ones, but there is also something new.

DAVID: And how would you characterize this new element?

FRITJOF: As far as the cultural situation is concerned, I can see two main new elements. One is the danger of destruction that is much greater than it ever was before. There is an actual possibility of annihilating ourselves, if we don't shift to the new paradigm. The paradigm shift is now really a question of survival for the human race. The other new aspect is a positive one. It is the feminist perspective. That simply was not there before.

DAVID: Probably if we were to look more closely, we could find many more new aspects. For instance, the fact that through mobility and through communications we are global now.

FRITJOF: Yes, the global awareness, the awareness of global interdependence. That's a new one, too, and it is very recent.

THOMAS: As far as theology is concerned, the dialectic between the new and the old is somewhat different from what it is in science. You said, David, that what we call the new theological paradigm is the recovery of our most ancient intuitions. This is true, and it is also where science and theology are methodologically distinct. The development of new theological paradigms does not entail the falsification of the "old" ones, any more than the adult involves the falsification of the child. But as Saint Paul said, "Now I have put childish ways behind me." The attempt to return to old theologies—and today many high-ranking ecclesiastics are trying to do so—falsifies the old. To teach sixteenth-century Catholicism at the end of the twentieth century is to betray the truth that really did find expression in that way four hundred years ago.

IV

**Criteria for
New-Paradigm Thinking
in Science and Theology**

FRITJOF: I would now like to discuss what we mean more specifically by new-paradigm thinking in science and theology. I have tried to identify five criteria of new-paradigm thinking, or systems thinking, in science, which, I believe, hold in all the sciences—the natural sciences, the humanities, and the social sciences. I formulated each criterion in terms of the shift from the old to the new paradigm, and you have identified five corresponding criteria of new-paradigm thinking in theology. I would now like to discuss each of these five criteria in some detail.

1 Shift from the Parts to the Whole

FRITJOF: The first criterion of new-paradigm science is the shift from the parts to the whole. In the old paradigm it was believed that in any complex system, the dynamics of the whole could be understood from the properties of the parts. In the new paradigm the relationship between the parts and the whole is reversed. The properties of the parts can be understood only from the dynamics of the whole. Ultimately there are no parts at all. What we call a part is merely a pattern in an inseparable web of relationships.

THOMAS: On the theological side is a corresponding shift from the parts to the whole. In the old paradigm it was believed that the sum total of dogmas, all basically of equal importance, added up to revealed truth.

83

In the new paradigm the relationship between the parts and the whole is reversed. The meaning of individual dogmas can be understood only from the dynamics of revelation as a whole. Ultimately revelation as a process is of one piece. Individual dogmas express particular insights into God's self-manifestation in nature, in history, and in human experience.

DAVID: I agree.

FRITJOF: That's one of the things I want to talk about. The shift that was so dramatic in physics in the 1920s was a shift from the view of the physical world as a collection of separate entities to the view of a network of relationships. What we call a part is a pattern in that network of relationships that is recognizable, because it has a certain stability. Therefore we focus our attention on it and we can then delineate it approximately and say, "This is what I call a cell," or an atom. But the decisive thing is that whenever you delineate this part and separate it from the rest, you make an error. You cut off some of the interconnections to the whole, physically or conceptually, and say, "This is now what I call a part. I know that it is related in this way and in that way to the rest, but I cannot consider all these connections, because it gets complicated." So I cut some of them off in the process of delineating the part.

DAVID: You just have to do that for didactic purposes.

FRITJOF: Yes, and the stability of the pattern allows you to do that. Now, in the old paradigm it was also recognized that things are interrelated. But conceptually you first had the things with their properties, and then there were mechanisms and forces that interconnected them. In the new paradigm we say the things themselves do not have intrinsic properties. All the properties flow from their relationships. This is what I mean by understanding the properties of the parts from the dynamics of the whole, because these relationships are dynamic relationships. So the only way to understand the part is to understand its relationship to the whole. This insight occurred in physics in the 1920s, and this is also a key insight of ecology. Ecologists think exactly in this way. They say an organism is defined by its relationships to the rest.

THOMAS: With regard to the parts, you said there are no parts at all?

FRITJOF: No *isolated* parts.

DAVID: That's the word I was going to suggest; maybe one should stress the word *isolated* here. We should also add a little footnote concerning the relationship between the whole and the parts in theology. Here it's the relationship between the process of revelation and the dogmas. The technical term *analogia fidei* sheds light on this relationship.

THOMAS: *Analogia fidei* (literally, "the analogy of faith") is the principle that says that you cannot talk about any one proposition of faith without implying all the others. There is never an understanding of a part, one doctrine or one teaching, isolated from the whole. The meaning is in the whole, it's not in a syllogism or a declarative sentence or whatever.

DAVID: That's quite remarkable, isn't it? It almost suggests a holographic model of theology.

FRITJOF: Yes, and it also reminds me of the bootstrap theory in particle physics, which says that each particle, in a certain sense, contains every other particle.

THOMAS: There is nothing particularly new about this principle. It's a cornerstone of medieval theology, but it carries special weight today.

The position of humans in nature

FRITJOF: In this connection I would like to touch on the relationship between humans and nature. Here a very useful distinction has emerged during the past two decades, the distinction between deep ecology and shallow ecology. In shallow ecology, human beings are put above nature or outside nature, and, of course, this perspective goes with the domination of nature. Value is seen as residing in human beings; nature is given merely use value, or instrumental value. Deep ecologists see human beings as an intrinsic part of nature, as merely a special strand in the fabric of life.

DAVID: Your distinction between deep and shallow ecology is a helpful one and very important to remember. Now the question arises, What then is the particular position of us humans in nature? It seems to me that we have a particular place and function. Every creature has its own, and so do we. I would like to ask you how the word *responsibility* might suit you to describe our particular function in nature. This word suggests itself because we are the ones who are responsible for what's happening. The peregrine falcons are not responsible for being endangered. Human beings are responsible. But we are responsible also for doing something to save endangered species.

FRITJOF: Let me say first that this whole question of anthropocentrism and the role of humans in nature is one that I find very challenging and very difficult.

The way I understand the deep ecologists, and systems theorists like Francisco Varela, for instance, is that they would say that every species has special characteristics, that you cannot talk about a "higher" and "lower" at all. Varela says he can't even talk about higher complexity, because there are so many aspects to complexity. In one aspect, obviously, the human organism is very complex. In another aspect, insects are very complex. So every species has its own special characteristics. To speak metaphorically, the bees would say that they are the crown of creation, and the dogs would say the same of their species, and so we say it of our species.

It seems to me this creates tremendous problems, or challenges, for theologians, because in conventional theology humans were always seen as being above and outside nature, destined to dominate nature.

DAVID: As I understand it, that is merely a cultural element of Christian tradition, not central to its message.

FRITJOF: But you know what I am talking about.

DAVID: Yes, I know exactly. I could give you terrible examples, particularly of the popularized version of this view.

In the image of God?

FRITJOF: So what does it mean, then, that man was created in the image of God? The animals were not created in the image of God, apparently. Or were they? Adam named them, and he was given domination over them. You know that whole story. How can you rephrase that in new-paradigm theology? Maybe we could begin by focusing on the notion of an immortal soul, which, as I understand it, is a uniquely human characteristic, according to Christian theology. Human beings are supposed to have an immortal soul, animals and plants supposedly not.

THOMAS: Again, who says?

FRITJOF: My religion teacher back in school.

DAVID: In the new paradigm, the right understanding of that story is that everything is created by the breath of God. "You give your breath to all creatures and they come alive."

THOMAS: "And you renew the face of the earth. If you withdraw your spirit, they die." Psalm 104.

DAVID: So "the spirit of the Lord," this breath, "fills the whole universe and holds everything together." That's a biblical statement; thus, all the plants and animals, everything, is filled with the life breath of God. It is explicitly stated in the case of humans, which concerns us most and where we know it from within. We humans are alive with God's own life, and we can know God, and we shall see God face to face.

FRITJOF: So the spirit of God, or the soul, is not a distinctive characteristic of humans.

DAVID: Not in biblical terms. That's a philosophical notion that comes much later. The concept of an immortal soul in the current sense is not strictly biblical.

FRITJOF: What about immortality and life after death?

THOMAS: The immortality of the soul is spoken of in one book in the Bible only, in the Old Testament, called the Wisdom of Solomon, which is, by the way, not even recognized by Jewish scholars or by Protestants. It's part of the Roman Catholic "canon" of Scripture; more precisely, it is called deuterocanonical, an inspired book added to the Hebrew Bible after it was translated into Greek.

DAVID: It's a thin trickle, and even the resurrection of Jesus has precious little, if anything, to do with the immortality of the soul. That is a Greek notion. It came into Christian tradition from Greek philosophy.

FRITJOF: But the resurrection is something distinctly human, isn't it? The plants do not resurrect.

THOMAS: On the contrary. That's the old paradigm, that your pets will not be in heaven. That's one of the most terrible things ever said to children! This is not theology. This is cultural baggage, a whole collection of trinkets that is not theology.

FRITJOF: So how do you interpret the credo that speaks about the resurrection of the flesh and eternal life? This is commonly understood as the exclusively human future, salvation.

DAVID: But only in popular opinion. Rightly understood, it means cosmic renewal.

FRITJOF: Can you say something more about that?

DAVID: First of all, we must take death much more seriously than it has been taken in the past. Much that has been said about the immortality of the soul is unbiblical. It was introduced later from other philosophical traditions and has thrown us off course. I want to take death as seriously as the Bible, particularly what we call the Old Testament, the Hebrew Bible. When you die, you're dead. Time's up for you, therefore there is nothing "after" death. Death is by definition that after which there is nothing. Time's up; your time has run out. Somebody else's time may go on, but your time's up. There is no "after" for you.

And yet we experience even now, before death, important moments that are not in time. They are, as T. S. Eliot says, "in and out of time." We experience here and now realities that are beyond time. In those moments time is experienced as a limitation. But when time's up for me, when time is over, all that is beyond time remains. It is not subject to change. It lasts. When my life is at last completed, it is like a fruit dropping off the tree. I do not go on and on forever doing things. Just as in my most alive moments in *this* life, I have all of my life at once.

Out of time, I possess my life. And since everything hangs together with everything in this "Now that does not pass away," we have everything. When time no longer separates us, we have all those whom we love, including all the animals and plants.

FRITJOF: Because we wouldn't be in our fullness if that weren't there.

DAVID: Right. Still, this remains at best a halting way of speaking about this fullness, about heaven and the "beatific vision," in which I as a Christian believe.

FRITJOF: What you just said sounds somewhat like the Bodhisattva idea in Buddhism, doesn't it? The Bodhisattva becomes enlightened when all other sentient beings are enlightened.

DAVID: Yes, it's related. SUNY has published an excellent anthology on *The Christ and the Bodhisattva,* edited by Steven Rockefeller. That book is worth reading in this context.

THOMAS: I haven't read the book yet, but on the basis of my own knowledge of Christianity and Buddhism, I would say that this is a good example of how the dialogue between two religions can bring out the best in both of them. Christianity, in its origins and development, has elaborated in great detail the social consequences of its spiritual doctrine. Buddhists have told me that this dimension of Christianity, though not lacking in Buddhist sources, has helped them develop their sense of responsibility to human society and to the Earth, as well as their awareness of the possibilities of Buddhism as a catalyst for social change. For our part, I can see the cosmic sensitivity of Buddhism and Hinduism as a stimulus for us, to discover in our own Scriptures and tradition the awareness of the nonhuman cosmos as part of God's plan of salvation. "Humans and beasts you save, O God!" says Psalm 36, one of the great mystical texts of the biblical Psalter; "With you is the source of life; in your light we see light." In the Christian tradition, I think everyone would recognize Saint Francis of Assisi as an "ecological" saint. He showed, in his life and in his poetry, how humans can not only be responsible for the nonhuman cosmos, they can also dialogue with it and respond to it.

FRITJOF: Now, if the immortal soul is not the distinctive feature of humanity, what is the new-paradigm version of creation and of the role of humans in nature?

THOMAS: There are many different formulations of this idea in the Bible. For instance, in chapter 8 of Saint Paul's letter to the Romans, he says that all creation is groaning as it awaits the revelation of the children of God, and we, too, groan with birth pangs. We're all bound up in this common condition which is considered painful. In other words, it's not a war of the humans against nature but rather a common awareness of something greater than all of us which is to be born, which is to be made manifest, at the end of time, at the end of history. The model that underlies chapter 8 of Romans is not that of chapter 1 of Genesis. There is also the theme of the Garden of Paradise in the Song of Songs, the symbolism of the new creation in the second part of Isaiah, and so on. You have all sorts of different statements about creation in the Bible, not just one.

FRITJOF: To get to the end of this topic in a reasonable time, I would be very happy just with a reformulation, without any footnotes, of the role of the human being in nature in terms of new-paradigm thinking.

THOMAS: What would be emphasized more today is the symbolism in Isaiah: "The lion shall lie down with the lamb. The little child shall put his hand in the lair of the viper." Here is a project for humanity today. The true human position is one where there is total harmony, where the human attitude is that of the child, of total ingenuousness. How do children relate to nature? They don't know how to fear nature, nor do they know how to dominate nature. The instinctive attitude of children toward animals, plants, trees is curiosity; they reach out, wanting to touch them, wanting to enjoy the beauty of it all.

DAVID: Do I understand you correctly? Would our human position be one of responsibility, after all? Are we to restore our world to that peaceable kingdom, to realize the myth of Paradise?

THOMAS: Rather than toiling to restore a mythical Paradise, our task, Isaiah seems to be saying, is to welcome the new era that God, the "source of life, in whose light we see light," is initiating. The prophecy of the lion and the lamb is closely linked to the birth prophecy: "Behold, a virgin shall conceive and be with child, and she shall call his name Immanuel, God-with-Us." First, welcome God's gratuitous gift of a new birth; then act accordingly.

FRITJOF: I would still like to hear from you, David, how you see the human position in nature.

DAVID: Well, let me try. First of all, how does anybody come to know about these things, the writers of the Bible included? From our human experience. Where have you and I experienced that we are made in the image and likeness of God? In our best, most alive, peak moments, because our whole notion of God comes from those moments. We discover there what we mean by God, if we want to use that term. We experience that we belong to God. Our true self is the divine self. This knowledge is anchored in mysticism. The Bible conveys that truth in the form of a story, in beautiful, mythical terms: we are earth, made of earth, breathing the divine life breath.

Then comes the part where we are put into the Garden "to tend it and keep it." That's where the sense of responsibility comes in. Stewardship, rather than exploitative domination, is the crux of that passage. Unfortunately the Book of Genesis has been misinterpreted and misused to justify a lot of destructive things. Rightly understood, Genesis says that Adam is put into the Garden to tend it and take care of it. So that is our responsibility.

The metaphor of the gardener

FRITJOF: Let's explore this metaphor of the gardener a little bit. The gardener is certainly, in a sense, above the garden or outside the garden. The gardener is not part of the garden. I remember a very witty definition of a weed, from a French gardener. He said, "A weed is anything I haven't planted." So the gardener is definitely outside the garden.

DAVID: Yes, I would say that the gardener is seen as separate from the garden. But this view is the result of the Fall. Our Fall, as it is described in that story, can be understood as the separation of the gardener from the garden. Before that, he didn't know that he was naked. This idea of nakedness has little to do with sexuality; it is the experience of estrangement: me over here and everybody looking at me.

That is the condition in which we find ourselves, alienated from the cosmos. But in Paradise we are presented as an integral part of the whole, at home in the cosmos.

FRITJOF: Now, earlier on you said that the human being, or Adam, is put into the garden to tend it and keep it. That was before the Fall.

DAVID: Yes, but the position of the gardener is not to be equated with a separation from the garden.

FRITJOF: Wait a moment. When you say "to tend it and keep it," you have the separation of the garden and the gardener.

DAVID: Distinction rather than separation. After all, the orange tree is distinct from the apple tree. The rabbit is distinct from the cabbage; here one even eats the other. Each does its own thing. And the thing that we humans do is to tend and keep nature. This is where I come back to the word *responsibility*.

FRITJOF: I'm still not happy with that, because you could say the dung of the rabbits also "tends" the garden, so to speak, by fertilizing the soil. When you look at ecosystems, you see that everywhere you have symbiotic relationships, you have a continual interchange of matter, cyclical pathways, and so on. What you observe then is that the ecosystem tends and keeps itself. From the scientific point of view, that's the very hallmark of life—self-organization. So the garden doesn't need anybody to tend and keep it, except now it does, because we messed it up so badly. So now we have the responsibility to tend and keep it.

DAVID: Well, try to imagine your own creation myth, parallel to that one. Imagine yourself being put into that garden, which is the cosmos. What would you do there?

FRITJOF: I would necessarily be integrated into it, because I would eat other living beings, and in the end I will be eaten by them. I will be part of the food chain. And I will take the various materials and use and cultivate them to build my home, to clothe and feed myself, to tend my young, as everybody else does. So I won't be any different. *Except*—now we come to the real difference—I will develop my *self*-consciousness. I will be able to reflect on myself, and I will develop language as a social phenomenon. And with language I will create together with my fellow humans the notion of an object, concepts, symbols, and culture.

DAVID: This is the part of the story where Adam gives names to the animals. You have described that part now. And now we have to see if there isn't in your own experience in the garden as you're projecting yourself into it also something that corresponds to the tending and keeping.

Maybe these words are just too much of a psychological block. Let me rephrase my question. You are in this garden. Could you envisage yourself putting fertilizer around certain fruit trees, since you know they will give you nicer fruit if you do that? I would think that would be typically human. Now, that would be the tending and keeping of the garden. Nothing more or less, it seems to me. Just making it grow well, and still perfectly within the ecosystem.

FRITJOF: You see, this is what Bateson calls purposive consciousness; it is a two-edged sword. As humans, with our intellect, our self-consciousness, our symbolic language, and all of that, we can project into the future. We can not only put fertilizer a little bit more on the right than on the left, which animals probably also can do, but we can actually project twenty years ahead and say, "Here I will plant something that will produce something in twenty years." So it's that part of our consciousness that will make us act differently. And if that then goes overboard and destroys the ecological wisdom that we share with all other creatures, then we get in trouble. And that's how we did get in trouble. And then the responsibility comes into the picture.

DAVID: In this sense, maybe responsibility comes in only later.

FRITJOF: Maybe the responsibility is precisely the *tempering* of the rational intellect, of the linear thinking by intuitive ecological wisdom.

THOMAS: As I listen to what you've been saying about the garden-gardener metaphor, I keep feeling uncertain whether we need to insist on the gardener model as essential to the Christian or Judeo-Christian view of the place of the human in the universe. The prophet Isaiah sees us not as gardeners involved in purposeful activity but as children engaged in play. And being a child doesn't mean doing nothing or being irresponsible; it does mean responding to the voices of creation, echoing these voices, and heeding their call.

DAVID: Yes, responsibility is a responsiveness, an ability to give an appropriate response.

FRITJOF: And the appropriateness of the response is not an issue with most other species, because they *have* the appropriate response. There's nothing inappropriate about how birds and plants respond to the environment. But a human response can be inappropriate, because we have purposive consciousness, and with it this ability to destroy nature and thus ourselves.

DAVID: I think now you have really put your finger on the sore spot. We certainly need not destroy nature, but we can. Other creatures can not. Only we humans have the frightful power to do so.

Freedom

FRITJOF: Right. And, of course, that's also where our freedom comes in.

DAVID: Yes. And freedom is the positive side.

FRITJOF: So freedom and responsibility go together.

DAVID: Exactly. That's the point. That is part of our experience; we must not sever the connection between freedom and responsibility.

FRITJOF: So our responsibility as the gardeners would be to reconnect ourselves to the garden, because we have separated ourselves and put ourselves above nature.

DAVID: And that was an aspect of the Fall.

FRITJOF: And not only that, we have also—how should I say it— secularized the garden and made it just a machine.

DAVID: We have de-spiritualized it.

FRITJOF: Killed it, in a sense.

DAVID: Yes, because the spirit is what gives life.

THOMAS: The spirit gives life, and the human spirit—whether with "purposeful consciousness" or "playful consciousness"—*can* give life. The destruction of the environment did not begin so much with the separation of the gardener from the garden as with the gardener's beginning to see the garden as a machine, subject to the operative will of the human in the driver's seat.

Could we return for a while to the topic of human freedom? Brother David, perhaps you might say a little more about it.

Individuality and personhood

DAVID: In connection with our freedom, it helps to distinguish between the individual and the person. An *individual* is defined by what distinguishes it from other individuals: so many individual eggs in this crate; so many human individuals in this population.

A *person* is defined by the relationship to others, to other persons and to other beings in general. We are born as individuals, but our task is to become persons, by deeper and more intricate, more highly developed relationships. There is no limit to becoming more truly personal.

So the challenge to our freedom would be to personalize the universe. Before we arrive, the world is not yet personal. Adam encounters in the Garden an impersonal environment, but now he can make it personal. His giving names to the animals is one aspect of this personalizing activity.

FRITJOF: That is even much stronger in the Native American traditions, where they not only give names but actual family relationships to all living things.

DAVID: Beautiful. And these myths are our common human heritage. They tell us what it means to be human.

FRITJOF: Frances Moore Lappé has said something very significant. When you define a person or personhood through the relationships to others, she says, this means then that my personal growth does not hinder yours. On the contrary, it enhances it. If I'm capable of relating more to everything around me, you will profit from it, because I can relate then more to you, and this will be your growth, and vice versa.

The conventional political idea of freedom, she says, is elbow room. If I grow, then you have to diminish, which is Newtonian: where one object is, another cannot be. The systemic view of growth and of freedom is one of mutual enhancement. There's no limit to it. It's not a zero-sum game.

THOMAS: The notion of political freedom as an instance of the Newtonian paradigm fascinates me. The contrast with the concept of freedom in the Gospels is striking. Political freedom involves pushing others aside to make room for yourself. But the freedom of Jesus is manifested above all in his self-diminishment. "He emptied himself, taking on the condition of a slave" (Philippians 2). John the Baptist said, "He must grow greater, while I must grow less."

DAVID: This insight has a negative implication, too, which you didn't mention. Anyone else's diminishment diminishes me. That is also something to remember in our world.

FRITJOF: At this point, we could try to connect what we have said about human nature and the role of humans in the cosmos to the shift of perception from objects to relationships, which is a general characteristic of new-paradigm thinking. This has now become clear to me for the first time, really. The way I can see it now is that we develop our personhood, our true nature through our relationships to others, but this is not peculiar to humans. It applies to all other living beings and, I would say, even to the patterns of inanimate matter. The internal characteristics of any pattern in nature are actually not internal at all. They are not intrinsic characteristics, but they are defined through the relationships to the rest of the environment. So the fact that our true nature arises from our relationships does not make us humans special or distinct from other living systems. What makes us special is our capacity for self-reflection, which brings with it language, concepts, abstract thinking. In addition to our great intellectual achievements, abstract thinking has given us the tendency of projecting linearly over large time spans, and such narrow purposive action, unfortunately, often leads us to destroy our environment and thus to destroy ourselves.

DAVID: But it also has made us capable of seeing purpose in contrast to meaning. We are capable not only of science but also of wisdom, not only of manipulating the workings of nature but of living our life in harmony with nature.

FRITJOF: Yes. Meaning is context. It is the way things fit into the larger whole.

DAVID: It is seeing each part in relation to the whole. And the key words are still *freedom* and *responsibility*. We can use or abuse our abstract thinking, while the other creatures around us, as far as we can see, do not have this freedom, for better or for worse.

FRITJOF: From the point of view of systems theory, living systems are self-organizing, and this means that they are autonomous. That autonomy is relative and gradually increasing as complexity increases. We humans have a special kind of freedom, which is the freedom of our inner world of concepts, and it's this kind of freedom that leads us into trouble.

THOMAS: I know this isn't what you mean, Fritjof, but I think some people regard our freedom of concepts and conscious choices as the source of evil. They would have us return to a "primitive" state of consciousness. But this isn't the way out. Trouble arises not from the complexity of our minds but from how we use the freedom that our ability to conceptualize the universe gives us.

God and nature

FRITJOF: Now that we have clarified our views on human nature, I'd like to shift the conversation to the nature of God, and especially to the contrast between the idea of an immanent God and that of a transcendent God. I think this is very important in our comparison of theology and science.

I mentioned the main discussion in ecological thinking today, which centers on the difference between deep and shallow ecology. One of the key points there is the role of humans vis-à-vis nature. Shallow ecology sees human beings as above or outside nature, whereas deep ecology sees human beings as a particular strand, one of many other strands, in the web of life. Related to this, I think, is the question of God in nature, God in creation, especially because human nature is supposed to be an image of God. So the relationship between humans and nature and between God and the creation seems to be parallel.

What I've always heard about Christianity, and what Gregory Bateson also emphasized, is that Christianity, although monotheistic, is also dualistic in its basic outlook, because it separates God from the creation. It has a transcendent God who stands opposite creation or dominates creation. He creates the world ex nihilo at the beginning, and then is always separate and always transcends the creation.

I've also often heard that mystics talk about their experience of an immanent God, something like Spinoza's *Deus sive natura* (God = Nature). It seems that this would be more the position of the deep ecologists, of a deep ecological theology, if you can call it that.

DAVID: We can make this word *God* serve a variety of purposes. If we take it, as we were striving to do, in a sense that representative spokespersons of all the theistic traditions can agree about, then we cannot say, God equals Nature. We speak about a horizon phenomenon when we speak about God. The horizon belongs inseparably to the landscape. There can't be a landscape without a horizon, nor a horizon without a landscape. But the horizon is not the landscape. The horizon recedes as you go and remains the horizon.

THOMAS: With regard to the assessment of Gregory Bateson that Christianity posits a dualistic framework, I would suggest that this is not really the genuine theological concept of divine transcendence. It's not that God is up there and the universe is down here. The image of horizon is excellent, because it suggests a context whose boundaries are continually receding. I would also suggest that God's transcendence is a transcendence inward. Saint Augustine invokes God by calling him *Deus intimior intimo meo,* "O God, closer to me than I am to myself, more intimate than my very innermost point." So it's a continually receding center of creation that is hidden within creation, a center that is everywhere but whose circumference is nowhere. Transcendence is also connected with the theme of *Deus absconditus,* the hidden God, as in Isaiah chapter 45: "Truly you are a God who hides himself, . . . who formed the earth and made it to be inhabited." Isaiah's hidden God is the maker of the Earth Household.

DAVID: Again, to tie this in with our own experience, out of which Augustine's statement comes, we experience our innermost reality, that which is closer to us than we are to ourselves, as in some way not simply ourselves but going beyond ourselves, just as the horizon recedes when we approach it.

FRITJOF: I think this is why psychologists call this experience trans-personal, because it goes beyond the personal.

DAVID: I would say, tentatively, what we today call transpersonal comes closer to what tradition really meant by transcendent than what the popularized version of transcendence suggests: some ethereal dimension above and beyond ordinary experience.

FRITJOF: That is fitting with what we said before, when you intro-duced God as the ultimate reference point of the religious experience. But if I say, "The universe is God," that's also transcendent, because it transcends me. So that doesn't answer the question, really. If you take creation as whole, is God the innermost, the ground of creation, the spirit of creation, the consciousness of creation, or something like that, or is God something that goes beyond that whole creation? I think that is the question. I use *creation* as a theological term; I wouldn't use it in other company. In other words, if I define the cosmos, or the universe, simply as everything that is, the question is, Does that include God or is God beyond everything that is?

DAVID: I have no pat answer to this question. But I would not want to answer it from the outside. The answer has to be found in our own expe-rience. We have to be able to know such things from within, not because somebody else tells us so. That is the principle. It may not always be pos-sible to carry it out, but in principle this is how we make the teachings of a given tradition our own. They have to be experientially anchored.

Now, let's check our own experience of reality. Say you pick up a pebble. You have a thing, but you also have a horizon, as it were. Do you know what I mean? Try it sometime. Pick up a pebble and just sit there looking at it for awhile. It has a horizon. When you really begin to see it, you realize it is silhouetted against something that is not seen. You can go through this experience with other objects, but a pebble is a good thing to start with. If you look at this pebble long enough, you will somehow experience that every "thing" is seen against a background of "nothing." You always perceive thing and nothing at the same time. If you didn't perceive the nothing, you wouldn't see the thing. Now, this nothing suggests what we mean when we speak about God. God is no-thing. That is why God is not nature. God is our horizon, the horizon of no-thing around everything. And that no-thing is much more important to us than all the things in the world together, because no-thing is *meaning*. Meaning is not a thing; it is no-thing, nothing. And God as Source of all meaning is . . . well, I'm reminded of what John Cage says, "Each something is a celebration of the nothing that supports it."

FRITJOF: But then, if I take this in the context of the new-paradigm perception of reality as an interconnected network, in which any object is defined by cutting it out from the rest, I can take your meditation on the pebble in the same sense. You cut out the pebble from the rest, and in everyday experience, you would think of it as a separate entity, but if you really meditate and reflect on it, you can bring yourself to experience the context, and then the pebble being set against that context. But what is that context from which you cut it out? It's the rest of the universe. So if you call that God . . .

DAVID: No, that was only one level. I used the experiment with the pebble as an illustration. But the pebble can stand for everything that is—for everything. And everything is perceived by us as something only because we silhouette it against nothing. And that nothing is what we mean when we talk about God as the source of meaning. Because we experience—and again I'm continually appealing to experience, it's all that matters—we experience in life only two kinds of encounters. We encounter either something or nothing. And that nothing of which I speak is meaning. That is far more important to us than anything, anything. Meaning is no-thing, and yet life without meaning, with all the things in the world, is not worth living.

FRITJOF: That nothing, no-thing, sounds to me like the Buddhist concept of *shunyata*.

DAVID: Right! What the Buddhists call *shunyata* comes as close as anybody can to speaking about God as horizon. Any Christian who is in dialogue with Buddhists should feel perfectly comfortable accepting *shunyata* as pointing toward God. After all, even the term *God* only points toward God. Of the horizon you never can say, "There it is." It's nothing. When you meet Buddhists on this common ground of no-thing, you can talk with them about God. I have experienced that more than once. When Buddhists recognize that you accept *shunyata*, emptiness, nothing, as that horizon which we happen to call God, it clicks. You continue to speak about "Ultimate Reality" and carefully avoid using the term *God*, but all of a sudden your Buddhist respondent starts using the term *God* quite comfortably. There is no problem anymore. We have met on the experiential ground of *shunyata;* the rest is just a matter of terms, you see.

It is what we mean, *meaning*, that is important. We use terms merely to point to this realm of meaning. And if the name God has any meaning, it points to the source of meaning, to that nothing which gives meaning to everything.

We should emphasize that in new-paradigm theology, the cosmos, God, and humans are all interrelated. Raimundo Panikkar, who is a kind of theologian's theologian, calls this the cosmotheandric principle. *Cosmos, theos, anthropos.* In other words, you cannot speak about God except in the context of cosmos and humans. You cannot speak about humans except in the context of God and the cosmos. You cannot even speak about the cosmos except in the context of God as the horizon and humans as the observers. All three belong together. That is the basis for what we call the new paradigm in theology.

THOMAS: What Panikkar calls the cosmotheandric principle is part of the basis, along with a theological model that, without being anti-rational, gives pride of place to what the earlier Christian tradition calls apophatic or "negative" discourse about God. The new theological paradigm is both holistic and apophatic. It sees God as the horizon of the universe but also as the ineffable Other.

FRITJOF: Now let me comment on this horizon metaphor. As you move, the horizon changes, so it is really not anything absolute. It's a concept that changes.

DAVID: It also implies what Dionysius the Areopagite, a most influential mystic writer of the early sixth century, said: "At the end of all our knowing, we shall know God as the unknown." He doesn't say, "Oh, don't bother, you will never know God." We shall indeed know God, but we shall know God as the unknown. The analogy is obviously taken from friendship: the more you know a friend, the more you know that friend as unknowable, as a mystery. This concept of mystery does not refer to what mystifies us, because we do *not yet* grasp it; and it refers to what we can *never* grasp because it is inexhaustible, as inexhaustible as life itself. Rilke reminded us that life was not a problem to be solved but a mystery to be experienced.

FRITJOF: Within the framework that you just laid out, how would you then answer the question, Is God immanent or transcendent? Can you answer it by using these two terms?

DAVID: Yes. I have done this before in a half-playful way, but I cannot say it better: God's transcendence is so transcendent that it even transcends our notion of transcendence and is therefore perfectly compatible with immanence. Again there is a paradox.

FRITJOF: But the transcendence refers to experience. Do I understand you right? God's transcendence transcends all our experience.

DAVID: Yes. Or, rather, our experience transcends all our concepts, even the concept of transcendence.

THOMAS: There is an experience of God that is beyond knowing, and the apophatic or negative language about God is its appropriate expression. The highest theological statements are all negative even when they are grammatically positive. "God is above all knowing and above all essence," said Saint John of Damascus. We cannot fit God into our concepts or words; we can use them, provided they do not attempt to represent God.

FRITJOF: Now, one of the main characteristics of the new systems theory of life is that it is not representational. It does not say an objective world exists out there, a reality that is then represented in our scientific theories. It says that in science we're bringing order and coherence into our experience. Actually, Maturana and Varela say that the process of cognition is a process whereby we "bring forth" a world in the act of cognition.

DAVID: That fits beautifully with theology, although not in its conventional formulation. I would not hesitate to say that the process in which the ordering of our experience creates the world, so to say, is an essential aspect of creation. We could say it is the Holy Spirit, God's consciousness within us, that creates the world. We are participating in the creation of the world by the very process of ordering our experience. This is how we experience God creating the world: we order our experience. Thus creation is happening at this very moment. And the ordering of our experience is what "tending the garden" really means.

FRITJOF: The reason I brought up this so-called constructivist position is that if you accept it, which I do tentatively, then you would have to say experience is all there is. We can talk only about experience and nothing else. So if God transcends all our experience, then he transcends everything we can talk about.

THOMAS: What you just said is a valid theological conclusion. In fact, our experience of God leads us to the point where it is no longer possible to speak about God. Silence is the only proper attitude.

DAVID: This is again the apophatic tradition in theology. One of its basic axioms is that everything that theology says about God, no matter how correct, is more false than it is true.

THOMAS: And that is a better definition of transcendence than any spatial metaphor. You see, part of the problem in philosophy and in a certain kind of second-rate theology is the confusion caused by the spatial metaphor—God out there or God over, above, or against. The real point about transcendence is that every statement about God implies its negation. This is what the transcendence of God means.

FRITJOF: Well, let me try something else that I have been playing with, an imagery that is connected with the theory of living, self-organizing systems. One of the key aspects of the theory is that the process of self-organization is a mental process. It was Gregory Bateson's great contribution to radically expand the concept of the mind. He said that mind is not a thing, it's a process. And this mental process is the process of self-organization, in other words, the very process of life. So at all levels the process of life is a mental process.

Now, when you get to the human level, you would say the human mental process has this very special property of self-awareness, of consciousness. Then when you go beyond that and take humanity as a whole, it would be a living system with its own mental process. That would be the collective consciousness. None of this has been really worked out in science. At the moment it is all very speculative.

THOMAS: It would be something like Teilhard de Chardin's noosphere.

FRITJOF: Exactly. Or Jung's collective unconscious. Teilhard, in fact, would be more relevant to going further beyond humanity to the planet. The noosphere as that planetary consciousness, the process of self-organization of the planet Earth.

Then you could go to the cosmos as a whole and say that cosmic consciousness is the self-organizing process of the entire cosmos. It has been speculated that this is what we mean by "God," the cosmic process of self-organization.

Now, if I put the question of transcendence versus immanence in that context, I could say that the fallacy has been that we think, Let's take the universe as a whole, and let's just add up everything that we know, all the trees and all the rocks and all the people. This sum total is the universe. Is God more than that or not? Now, that's a fallacy, because we are clearly not talking about the universe as a whole. The universe is a self-organizing, living entity; therefore it's all the trees and rocks and people, but these are just patterns. More important are the principles of organization of that whole. And these principles of organization are not something material.

DAVID: That's the nothing of meaning that I was talking about.

FRITJOF: Right. So if I say then, God is the sum total of these principles of organization at the cosmic level, of the cosmic process of self-organization, then the answer to the question of transcendence or immanence will depend on what I call the universe. If I call the universe everything that exists, including all processes, ideas, and so forth, God is *immanent* in the universe. But if I say that the universe is all the *things*

I know, all the trees and rocks and all the stuff in the universe, the structures, then God clearly transcends that, because it's the principles of organization that hold it all together and, you could very well say, that create it. That's self-creation, self-organization.

DAVID: That's a good approach. It seems to hold many possibilities.

THOMAS: What relationship does your concept of the principles of organization or self-organization in the cosmos have with the idea of a world soul, which is a very classical, Platonic notion?

FRITJOF: I would say the difference is that this theory of self-organization is much more sophisticated than anything we have seen before in the sciences. For example, it says that creativity is inherent in life. The process of self-organization is an inherently creative process. The creation of novelty is one of the hallmarks of life. Any living system creates novelty all the time; it goes through a path of creating novelty, which is called ontogeny, the path of individual development. Then the species goes through phylogeny, the evolutionary path, which again creates novelty all the time. So creativity is an essential part of self-organization. And therefore, I believe, you can relate it to the notion of creation in theology. If you see it cosmically, then that comes very close to what you said before.

DAVID: Yes, I like it. As you continue to work it out, it may be an example of what has happened in the past: someone coming from an attempt to explain the world from a scientific point of view ends up in theological statements. That is a valid way. You are working toward a theological understanding that could become fruitful. What you are describing here is creation, and theology has always held, even in the old paradigm, that creation is an ongoing process here and now. If it weren't that, everything would collapse.

    If God is the life of the world, you have just given an account of the life of the world, from a very different perspective.

FRITJOF: It has a lot of connection points, but the one thing that probably makes theologians uncomfortable is that the key notion is *self-organization*. The universe organizes itself, and therefore it's also *self-creating*.

DAVID: A theologian like Panikkar does not hesitate to speak in a highly sophisticated way of the cosmos as God's body, as do process theologians, such as John B. Cobb, Jr. That notion, he claims, has been misunderstood but not really rejected in theology.

FRITJOF: You see, this would be a very straight parallel to another statement of this theory of self-organizing systems, that the relation between matter and mind is one of structure and process. The structure, of course, is what we commonly mean by the universe in all the things we see. The process would be its consciousness.

The personal God

FRITJOF: Okay, I have another question that puzzles me. What do you mean by a "personal God"? Remember, we spoke about revelation being tied to a personal God. I want to put this question in the context of personhood being defined through our relationships to others. How does this work with the concept of God? What does it mean that God is "personal"?

DAVID: Let us first say that it does not mean that God is a person. The Christian tradition believes that God is one in three persons and, from that moment on, of course, "person" has a different meaning from what we normally mean by person.

THOMAS: When we say that God is personal, we mean that we can and do have a real relationship with God as the Ultimate Reality to which we belong. We have a real relationship in which we fully realize our personhood, and that's the sense in which we talk about the "personhood" of God. But when Christian theology speaks of the "Persons" of the Trinity, it means something quite different: that the very essence of God is relational, and that the three persons in God are not "individuals" but "subsistent relations," existing only in and for one another.

DAVID: I would recommend Schubert Ogden in this context. He's a leading Protestant theologian whose work I have long been impressed and inspired by. He speaks of God as the one who makes a difference to everything and to whom everything makes a difference. God does not live in splendid isolation but cares—cares for every creature with affectionate love, for lilies, sparrows, humans. God is personally inter-related with every creature through compassion.

THOMAS: Buddhism affirms that the ultimate reality is emptiness; it also affirms that the ultimate reality is infinite compassion. The great intuition of Mahayana Buddhism is the identity of emptiness and com-passion. I think this is the Buddhist affirmation that comes closest to the "God is personal" statement in the theistic religions.

DAVID: Absolutely. Long before we are even theists or nontheists we all experience in our best, most alive moments that we belong. The notion of our ultimate belonging implies that to which we ultimately belong. But it's at this point no more than a direction, and those who use the term *God* correctly use it for that direction.

And now begins what Christopher Fry calls exploration into God. That's the great human enterprise that has been going on ever since there have been humans and still engages every one of us, whether we are aware of it or not. It's our deepest quest. We search for meaning, we search for belonging, and that means that we are all exploring God-territory. But that territory is so vast that you can go on forever and ever exploring one part of it and never meet other groups that explore other parts. There are certain crossroads where you choose to go in a certain direction. After that, you are not likely to reach the territory others are exploring who took a different turn.

One of those crossroads is the discovery that belonging is mutual. If we belong to God, God belongs to us; we are in a relationship. This is mysticism of course, but any one of us can experience it daily. God is related to us in a personal way. That's the experiential basis for the notion that God must have all the perfection that makes me a person and none of the limitations.

FRITJOF: How is this connected with personhood arising from rela-tionships? The richer my relationships, the richer I am as a person.

DAVID: I realize my belonging, which makes me a person, only in lim-ited ways with a few people, things, plants, and animals, and not very deeply. But when we are talking about the horizon, the one who is beyond everything, we conclude that God has to be personally related to everything and in the most intimate depths.

FRITJOF: What bothers me here is this: I accept your definition of a person, that a person is defined through relationships. The more related we are, the richer is our personhood. So then you say, "Alright, God is related to everything." So God has the richest personhood you can imagine. Actually it's so rich that it transcends everything we can imagine, because being related to everything already transcends what we can imagine. So far, so good. But this relationship that God has is always to part of himself. It's not to something else. Whereas the relationships we have, what constitutes our person, are relationships to what is distinct from ourselves. So if a person arises from relationships to what is outside that person, that cannot very well be taken as an analogy to God as a person. That's what I want to get at.

DAVID: Ah, this is great! At this point your own thinking brings you close to answering the question you raised earlier, Why speak of God as Trinity? Now you put your finger on the decisive spot when you say, God does not relate to something else. In our deepest relationship to God, God ultimately relates to God's own self. We are aware of this in our mystic moments. The true self of ourselves that is related to God is simply God-in-us. This experience implies that you can speak of God as Trinity: God-in-us, who constitutes our innermost self; God as horizon, to whom we are ultimately related; and God as the living relationship between those two poles, our very life. Those are of course not three but one God.

All speculation about the Trinity is ultimately based on mystic experience. Lesser theologians may sometimes merely juggle concepts, but the great theologians always knew that we take part in God's very life. What we can not say is that we are part of God. For what we call God is too simple to have parts. That's why we speak of things, plants, animals, humans not as parts of God but as so many words of God. That's what the Bible means when it says of the whole universe, "God spoke and it came into being."

God as ultimate horizon holds everything together. In this sense, God is the great "Yes" to belonging that holds everything there is together. But this is another way of saying "God is love." Love is precisely this: the "yes" to belonging. This "yes" is the word lovers say to each other. It is the most creative of all words.

Actually God is also too simple to speak many words. It's rather as if the love that is God expressed itself "from before always" in one word so full that it needs to be spelled out in countless ways, ever anew. That spelling out of God's love is one way of understanding creation. Each one of us is in this sense a new way of spelling out God's one word. But here we make the exciting discovery that we are not only spoken but spoken to by God.

So *shunyata,* God, nothing, the great silence, finds expression in one word that is so perfect that it says everything and can be understood with ever-new meaning by God's own self-understanding, within *us,* as we said. Thus we ourselves are deeply engaged in this relationship: through us humans this world consciously takes part in the triune life of God.

Silence, word, and understanding are "persons" of the one God, yet obviously not in the sense in which we ordinarily speak of persons. Have I boiled this down to the point where it is just too highly condensed?

FRITJOF: Well, it's pretty heady stuff.

DAVID: To bring it down from the head into experience, we have to come back to where it all started, with the experience of a particular human being called Jesus. Out of his Jewish tradition he related to God with great intimacy, like a son to a father, and allowed his whole life to be shaped by this relationship, by the Holy Spirit of God. That means he went a long way beyond conceiving of God merely as an impersonal horizon. His followers enter, together with Jesus, into this personal relationship to God and speak of Father, Son, and Holy Spirit as "persons" of the Trinity. Of course, only "the Son" is a *human* person, and that's what person means for us, today. Part of it is a problem of language.

FRITJOF: I must say that this discussion of the personal God is still something I don't really grasp.

DAVID: Would it be possible to say where your difficulty lies?

FRITJOF: Let me try this. If you say your personhood arises from your relationship to others, then the richer these relationships are, the richer your person becomes. So you talk about your relationships to other people, and as a deep ecologist you would extend them to the whole living nature, to the cosmos as a whole. It's a tremendous richness. The more you extend it, the richer your person becomes. For none of this do I need a personal god, at least in the sense that I still understand it. A Buddhist attitude is completely sufficient for me.

DAVID: That Buddhist attitude can be an important corrective to the Christian understanding of God as personal. The two balance each other. I'll say more about that in a moment, but first let me clarify this: Personhood arises not only from relationships to others but also from relationship to self. We possess ourselves in freedom; we are challenged to be faithful to our innermost self; those are also ways in which we experience the existential relatedness from which personhood arises.

Now when you speak of the Buddhist attitude, let's remember what Thomas said earlier about the Buddhists' identifying emptiness with compassion. He was right when he located there the Buddhist approach to the truth that Christians speak of as God's being personal. I have been able to verify this in conversation with eminent Buddhists, even with the Dalai Lama. I say, "Well, you speak of compassion mostly as an attitude you show toward others. Yet, long before you can be compassionate to anyone else, you receive compassion. When you trace the compassion you receive back to its source—emptiness—you know what we Christians mean when we say 'God has loved us first.'" Buddhists are a bit puzzled by this, but they like the approach.

I suppose that as long as we move on the level of speculation, we never get it, neither in its Buddhist nor in its Christian expression. But in prayer and meditation we can experience it.

Patriarchal images

FRITJOF: I have to mention something else that is relevant here, but it's a big subject and we're not going to do it justice. If we speak about God as a person, we have to use gender, and traditionally Christianity, being a patriarchal religion, has used the male gender. This is a tremendous difficulty. First, it's a great injustice, but I think it's also a tremendous difficulty theologically. We associate with the Father a position of separateness, loyalty, obedience, opposition, whereas we associate with the image of the Mother an embeddedness, unconditional love, and so on. Feminist theologians have pointed out repeatedly that the female image is much more appropriate from an ecological point of view.

DAVID: That is an important observation, and we have to try to find a new language. We are still culturally bound in this respect. The cultural wrappings of the tradition make things difficult, but the tradition itself is greater and deeper than the cultural wrappings. For instance, right in the Book of Genesis it says that God created humans in God's own image, "male *and* female God created them."

THOMAS: And this implies that it is the couple which is the image of God, and not the individual.

FRITJOF: Nevertheless, the entire Catholic hierarchy consists of men, and God is always male. This is a whole area that we won't even be able to go into, but it needs to be a part, and I think an extremely important part, of the new paradigm in theology.

DAVID: Yes, and fortunately more and more women theologians are working on this today.

THOMAS: The whole issue of women in the Church emerges in a new light now. It will have to be addressed in connection with the total paradigm shift, in the human sciences, and in theology.

DAVID: It's about time!

FRITJOF: How do you deal with this personally when you speak and write? I find it impossible to use the term *God* because of this patriarchal baggage, and I do find "God" as "she" very unnatural and artificial.

DAVID: I sometimes use the word *she* when I refer to God. But, normally, when I'd have to say the word *he* or *she* or *it,* I try to repeat the word *God.* God creates us in God's own image, for instance. Not in his image or her image, but God creates in God's image. So I repeat the term. This is one of scores of other little tricks that you have to use. You have to take a social stance against the injustice in the Church and in the Christian tradition that is still keeping women down. We do that in the monastery and do it individually. Many monastic and other communities are now retranslating the texts; you can take out the "he" and put in other terms.

For example, the Psalms, which are used daily in worship, were completely retranslated in a nonsexist language and are now used in that form. But it is a very thorny issue that we have to keep working on.

THOMAS: It's a sociological, theological, and spiritual problem. I'm beginning to realize that some of the qualities in Jesus that we recognize as divine, in fact quite a majority of them, are classifiable as typically feminine qualities—compassion, tenderness, mercy, relatedness, attention to the individual. You can go down the list.

DAVID: Also we should not want to project today's notion of father into the term *father,* as Jesus applied it to God. When Jesus speaks about a father, most typically, the father of the prodigal son, this father acts in every way like a dear Jewish mother. He sees his son coming from afar, rushes to meet him and exclaims "Oh, my son! Just look at you! You're thin as a bone. Your clothes are filthy and falling apart! Come! Let me feed you, give you new clothes, put a ring on your finger!" And he goes and prepares a huge dinner. And all that is the father! All that is what Jesus means when he says, "Father."

FRITJOF: Jewish society at that time, though, was a full-blown patriarchal society.

DAVID: It was, and it is historically well established that Jesus made enemies by treating women as equals, which was not accepted in society.

FRITJOF: On the other hand, one also has to recognize that the traditional father image is now changing. My daughter, who is now two, does not have the image of a distant father at all. In her daily life she is equally attached emotionally to both of us. When she wakes up at night, she will cry "Daddy" as often as "Mommy." It's completely equal.

DAVID: When she grows up and hears God called father, she will not be in that bind. But we, because we have this stereotype of what the father is like, as you very well described it, when we speak of God as father, we immediately think that we have to earn God's love. In our stereotype a father will love you on condition that you shape up, whereas a mother loves you unconditionally. Since we never speak of God as mother, we forget that the heart of the Christian message, the good news, is that God loves us unconditionally. You don't have to earn God's love.

"In the image of God?"

FRITJOF: We have talked about the role of humans in nature and about our image of God. In what sense now are *we* created in the image of God?

DAVID: We have some idea of what God is like. In what ways do we really resemble God? I would say that we do not know what God is like, except in our best moments, to which we always have to return in this context. In our mystical moments we know that we have touched the divine as our own innermost self. And that is what is meant by being created in God's image and likeness.

THOMAS: Exactly. This is the proper theological understanding. That article of faith, that we are created in the likeness of God, states not that we are comparable to God in some way but that we have a relationship with God, which is incomparable but which is something that is given with our very existence. It is a mystery, but it is a reality we can discover if we go to the very depth and center of our being.

However, it is not simply a static reality. The Eastern Christian tradition posits a tension between the static and dynamic dimensions of this relationship by using in a distinct way the term *image* and *likeness*. We are made in the image of God. In other words, we are constituted in the possibility of intimate, mystical relationship with God, and then we grow into likeness. There is a progressive unfolding of the image within human life.

FRITJOF: The term *image* is then misleading. If I draw an image of a flower, this will be an outline of the flower that will have some of its characteristics but not all. Not very many in fact.

THOMAS: The comparison is not with an image that you draw. In the Bible the term suggests that the relationship is similar to that of a child to the parent. The child is not a tracing, not a xerox copy of the parent, but is the parent's image and likeness.

FRITJOF: Oh, I see. That's where it comes from.

THOMAS: It is a new life that has the parent's life as its origin.

DAVID: The word that is used in Hebrew is the same word that in other passages is translated as "idol." Much of the Hebrew Bible, and the New Testament for that matter, continually inveighs against idol worship. The only place this word for idol is used in a very positive sense is where we're told that we are created as God's idol. In other words, we are the only representations of God.

FRITJOF: But the idol is like the image of the flower. It is a statue that is a work of art representing the divine.

THOMAS: I think the use of the term is paradoxical. The fact that it's the only positive usage suggests a subtle element of typical Hebrew irony here. Ultimately, if one is to worship God, one must turn to the human; in other words, one must turn to one's own heart.

DAVID: But it points also to a great difference between the philosophical God of whom we have a clear notion and the biblical God of whom we can say only that this God is in some way like us. In living, we discover that God reality, not in a static way but in a living way, by becoming ourselves. One of the earliest statements in Christian theology claims that "the glory of God is man and woman fully alive." Our aliveness images God's aliveness. Perhaps this is how we can paraphrase in contemporary terms the statement that we are created in the image and likeness of God. Aliveness is the point of comparison behind the notion of "image."

FRITJOF: Maybe we could compare this in some sense to falling in love, because when you have a peak experience—certainly falling in love is a kind of peak experience—what you discover is that this person touches something in you, moves something. There is a resonance, it strikes a chord. In some very deep sense, he or she is like you, and you are like him or her. So this is likeness in terms of a resonance, maybe. And resonance, of course, is a dynamic phenomenon. The experience of that resonance is a peak experience.

DAVID: And what you experience in those moments when you fall in love is not only that the other one is like you, but half of the excitement is that the other one is so totally different from you and that these two paradoxically coincide. Somebody who is really totally other is so totally like me, and that is also mirrored in our relationship to the divine. On the one hand, we know God as our innermost self, and on the other hand, as the absolutely other, as the altogether other.

THOMAS: The essence of mysticism, in my opinion, is that these two experiences coincide.

Let me interject another theological thread that is related to the concept of the human as the image of God and that perhaps has been forgotten in theology: the human as the image of the universe, as the image of the total created reality. A very simple expression of this is found in Saint Gregory the Great. He says that the human being has something of the angels, something of the birds, something of the flowers, something of the stones.

DAVID: Is that what we call the microcosm?

THOMAS: Yes. It is, of course, the classical idea of the human as microcosm reflecting the macrocosm or the total reality. I think it also suggests that human self-realization is possible only in so far as one becomes conscious of this fundamental relatedness with every element of the cosmos, with every element of creation.

FRITJOF: The idea of the human being as a microcosm reflecting the macrocosm is, of course, very old. It is known as the hermetic tradition. This idea also exists in modern science as the similarity of patterns. Gregory Bateson coined the phrase "the pattern which connects." That is the pattern we have in common with the cosmos. In this connection I always think of a very beautiful phrase of Goethe: If the eye were not sunlike, it could never perceive the sun. There's a connection. The way we would rephrase this in scientific terms today is that we are intimately connected with what we observe. We bring something to our observation. What we observe depends on how we look at it, and that whole connection is a connection of pattern.

2 Shift from Structure to Process

FRITJOF: The second criterion for new-paradigm thinking in science is a shift from structure to process. In the old paradigm it was thought that there were fundamental structures and then there were forces and mechanisms through which these interact, thus giving rise to processes. In the new paradigm every structure is seen as a manifestation of an underlying process. The entire web of relationships is intrinsically dynamic.

THOMAS: On the theological side, this would correspond to a shift from revelation as timeless truth to revelation as historical manifestation. In the old paradigm it was thought that there was a static set of supernatural truths that God intended to reveal to us, but the process by which God revealed them was seen as of little importance. In the new paradigm the dynamic process of salvation history is itself the great truth of God's self-manifestation. Revelation as such is intrinsically dynamic.

DAVID: Is that emphasis on the dynamic clear? Formerly we thought what mattered were clearly articulated articles of faith. Now we realize what really matters is our interaction with the divine reality. Here and there we catch a glimpse that is clear enough so that we can articulate it. But the articulation always falls short of the reality we experience. So the experiential process of interacting with the divine is what counts, the walking along the road, not the milestones.

Spirit and matter

FRITJOF: I see. Yes, that's very clear to me. Let me now turn to a particular kind of processes, the processes of life. In the new theory of living systems, the processes of life are seen as being essentially mental processes. In fact mind is defined as a process. In this theory the relationship between mind and matter is one between process and structure. There is no mind without matter. The two are complementary. So any kind of phenomenon where you have free-floating spirits without a material complement would be impossible. What does this do to the notion of a divine spirit without any matter?

DAVID: Spirit means life. It is the life of something. And according to Panikkar, this notion of spirit as totally unrelated to anything material is just a philosophical aberration that cannot do justice to reality. Karl Rahner, *the* Catholic theologian of this century, is certainly a cautious thinker, yet he, too, is reluctant to accept any notion of spirit unrelated to matter. For me spirit and matter are two sides of the same coin, two interwoven aspects of reality.

THOMAS: The opposition between spirit and matter, central to the thought of Descartes, falls with the fall of the old paradigm in general.

DAVID: Does that include old–paradigm theology as well?

THOMAS: Yes, along with every other theory of the "soul" as a disembodied substance. For me a *created* spirit separate from matter is inconceivable. Matter is that which gives direction to the mental process. There cannot be a mental process that simply floats in the void. As for the notion of *God* as spirit, I think it's simply another way of addressing the whole question of transcendence. When one has a proper concept of transcendence, one speaks of God as Spirit. But this does not mean that God has, or is, a "mental process." God transcends *both* spirit and matter, or, as Saint John of Damascus said, "God is beyond names and beyond essence."

Self-organization

FRITJOF: The funny thing about the concept of self-organization is that it can be presented as having a "trinitarian" nature. These are the aspects: the pattern of organization, the structure, and the process.

The pattern of self-organization is the totality of relationships that define the living system's essential characteristics. This pattern can be described in an abstract way without referring to energy, physical substances, organisms, and so on, without using the language of physics and chemistry. It's an abstract pattern of relationships.

The structure of a living system is the physical realization of this pattern. The same pattern may be realized in different biological structures (a cell, for example, or a leaf or a flower), and these structures are described in the language of physics and chemistry.

The error most biologists make today is to work on the structure level and to believe that by knowing more and more about the structure, they will eventually know life. But, they will never know what life is as long as they limit themselves to its structural aspects. Only when they also take into account the pattern will they be able to really grasp the phenomenon of life.

Now, the continual realization of the pattern of self-organization in a specific biological structure involves a dynamic process, the life process. It involves the continual self-renewal of the organism, adaptation of the environment, learning, evolution, and so on. And this life process, according to Bateson, is essentially a mental process. That's the third part.

DAVID: Once you step from your pattern into the process of its realization, how do you avoid the idea that by studying, for instance, neurophysiology, you will come to understand psychological processes?

FRITJOF: You can not derive the pattern from the structure. You have to study and understand it independently. You see, I can tell you whether a given system is self-organizing or not. But if you give me the condition that I will have to stick to the language of physics and chemistry and not go beyond it, then I won't be able to tell you. I have to go beyond the material aspect and speak about abstract patterns of relationships.

The Trinity

DAVID: I would suggest that one could explore in this context the basic theological statement that the only thing that allows us to speak of a diversity of persons within a triune God is relationships.

FRITJOF: The reason I said this is a trinitarian theory is that process can quite clearly be associated with spirit. Structure can clearly be associated with the word made flesh. And the pattern of organization, or the principle of organization, would then be associated with the Father, I suppose.

DAVID: The word made flesh is also called the image of the invisible God. The invisible is the pattern for the visible.

FRITJOF: It's an intriguing parallel.

THOMAS: It could be just as legitimate a parallel as others that have been used in the past, such as the psychological parallels used by Saint Augustine: Father as memory, Son as intellect, Spirit as will. With this new metaphor, we would have to speak about a history of *cosmic* salvation as well.

Evolution, teleology

FRITJOF: The other concept I would like to discuss in this context is evolution. When we talk about the processes of life, they lead to a path of development, both for individual organisms and in the evolution of the species.

The theory of self-organization says that there is no goal in this path. It is called a drifting. Maturana and Varela, two of the leading researchers in this field, talk about an ontogenic drift and a phylogenic drift. This drifting is a continual mental response to environmental influences. Creativity at every step. This is why two organisms will develop in different directions and will have different individualities or different personalities. But there's no plan, there's no blueprint, and there's no direction.

DAVID: Do you buy that?

FRITJOF: I haven't formed an opinion.

DAVID: No plan, fine. No blueprint, even better. But no direction? I find that really problematic.

THOMAS: Is there any consistent consensus on this? Are there others who see it in a more teleological way?

DAVID: Teleology is a dirty word for many scientists today. But I do believe that in some form it is needed here. Without direction toward a goal, we just can't account for the phenomena we observe. Unless we see that purposefulness is present even in the subatomic particles, we risk putting humans way up there, above nature. We humans know purpose, we act purposefully. Does that set us apart from the rest of nature? I don't think so.

But I noticed that you reacted strongly to what I said, Fritjof.

FRITJOF: What does that mean, purposefulness?

DAVID: That you somehow envisage a goal and then strive for it. The opposite of drift.

FRITJOF: The way I see it, personally, is that when you look at an organism in an environment, you observe that it develops, it moves along, and then you ask whether it has purpose or is just drifting. Now, if you switch from that level to a larger level, you see that the movements of the smaller organisms are part of the pattern of organization of the larger system. That seems quite evident to me.

For example, if you see a single blood cell in my veins and follow it, it will drift along; you won't be able to predict anything. But if you study the body as a whole, you might say, "I injured my finger and now my immune system is reacting." There's a global response to the injury and this is why this blood cell goes there. It's quite evident to me that the movement and development of one part is part of the pattern of organization of the larger system. In that sense I can see a purpose.

DAVID: That will satisfy me. But I can not accept the notion that by blind drifting, by pure chance, we arrive at something as complex as an eye, for instance.

FRITJOF: Well, they do not talk about chance, like Jacques Monod. It's all mindful, a mental response, a coevolution of organism and environment with the environment also being alive.

DAVID: At any rate, what you said does satisfy me. Formerly, if I understand you correctly, the old paradigm in science started from the bottom of unrelated things, which eventually worked their way up to a marvelous harmony in which all hangs together, this beautiful dance. Now you start from the top, the goal, the *telos,* the whole. That's an altogether different story.

FRITJOF: That's right, because you have to understand the dynamic of the whole in order to understand the properties of the parts. But let me pursue the notion of purpose a little further. I remember Joseph Campbell emphasizing repeatedly that eternity is not "a long time"; it's outside time.

DAVID: As Augustine defines it, "the now that does not pass away."

FRITJOF: When you are in this kind of mode, how can you talk about purpose? In a now that doesn't pass away, how can there be purpose?

THOMAS: Exactly. God has no purpose. God simply is.

DAVID: But in time, we have unfolding of meaning.

FRITJOF: I think we're doing a balancing act here at the limits of factual language. In poetry there is no problem. Take, for example, the famous Blake line "Hold infinity in the palm of your hand."

DAVID: This is the widest context, but I'm still concerned with a certain direction. Saint Augustine says that everything is drawn by its love; we love what attracts us. Since I see this so clearly in us humans, I am inclined to think that it didn't come in with us or even with the animals, it must have been there in the plant world and even in the world of matter.

FRITJOF: No, I think it does come in with human consciousness. We spoke about consciousness and purpose before.

THOMAS: Yes we did, in the context of the Bible, which always connects "purposefulness" with the notion of "time." Interpreters and theologians usually speak of the Bible's "linear" view of time. But this is just one metaphor; another is that of time as a great void that is filled up, so that it assumes a greater and greater density. We read that Christ came "in the fullness of time," and that the victory of love, of life over death, will also come "in the fullness of time." This view of time and hence of purpose is not directional, nor is it linear, yet it is equally valid theologically.

FRITJOF: Previous cultures, and tribal cultures even today, had a much more cyclical notion of time, which was gleaned from nature. What I always heard was that it was a characteristic of the Christian tradition to posit the birth of Christ as a marker and then count linearly from that to the resurrection of all creation as the endpoint.

THOMAS: As we do in the common calendar, counting backward B.C. and forward A.D. This again is one metaphor.

FRITJOF: But how does theology differ today? That is the interesting question to me.

THOMAS: On this point there is no unanimity among theologians. However, I find Teilhard de Chardin's hypothesis of the "Omega point" quite intriguing. Time and purpose converge at a point beyond the human, which Teilhard identifies with the cosmic Christ.

DAVID: It is important to me that we not insist so much on limiting the Christian message to its historic framework. What we Christians see as the divine expressing itself in the cosmos, but particularly in human history, must be accessible to all human beings in one form or another. It may be expressed in cosmic rather than historic terms by traditions that are not so interested in history.

THOMAS: I think that's quite true, and I think that we are facing an opportunity for theology that is comparable only to that in the earliest period of Christianity, when, between one persecution and another, Christians opened themselves, with a remarkable degree of freedom and intellectual acuity, to the great philosophical currents of the ancient world. Today we have an equally golden opportunity for theological creativity.

DAVID: And now we are dealing not only with the Hellenistic Mediterranean world but with the whole world.

THOMAS: With the whole world, and with cultures that may have more to offer us than Hellenistic culture offered to the great early Christian writers. The accessibility of Hindu and Buddhist texts, in the original languages and in good translations, constitutes an opportunity that is incomparably greater than what Saint Irenaeus and Saint Justin or, later, Saint Basil and Saint Gregory of Nyssa had with the philosophical currents of their own day.

DAVID: Do you see signs that we are beginning to avail ourselves of those opportunities?

THOMAS: Well, there are signs that we are beginning, but just signs and just beginning.

3 Shift from Objective to "Epistemic" Science

FRITJOF: My third criterion for new-paradigm thinking in science is a shift from objective science to what I call epistemic science. In the old paradigm scientific descriptions were believed to be objective, that is, independent of the human observer and the process of knowledge. In the new paradigm it is believed that epistemology, the understanding of the process of knowledge, has to be included explicitly in the description of natural phenomena. At this point there is no consensus about what is the appropriate epistemology, but there is an emerging consensus that epistemology will have to be an integral part of every scientific theory.

THOMAS: On the theological side that would correspond to a shift from theology as an objective science to theology as a process of knowing. In the old paradigm theological statements were assumed to be objective, that is, independent of the believing person and the process of knowledge. The new paradigm holds that reflection on nonconceptual ways of knowing—intuitive, affective, mystical—has to be included explicitly in theological discourse. At this point there is no consensus on the proportion in which conceptual and nonconceptual ways of knowing contribute to theological discourse. But there is an emerging consensus that nonconceptual ways of knowing are integral to theology.

DAVID: May I ask you a question, Fritjof, to start us off? You say that, at this point, there is no consensus on what is the proper epistemology. Yet you have dealt with this question for a while now, and I'm sure you have given lots of thought to it. Would you have a hunch about the direction in which one ought to be looking for that epistemology?

FRITJOF: I think the people who are on the forefront of this research tend to say that a school known as "constructivism" is the appropriate epistemology. It says that what we observe is not a world that exists objectively and is then represented but is rather a world that is created in the process of knowing. As Maturana and Varela say: "The world is *brought forth* in the process of knowing."

DAVID: It's amazing that so long ago there was an anticipation of this insight through myth: God speaks the Word that expresses God's knowing, and in that process God creates the world. I think there's a real parallel. Then, it was a kind of theology through myth. Now a similar idea—that the mind brings forth things in the process of knowing—is emerging from scientific thinking.

FRITJOF: The way I understand this whole thing about bringing forth the world is not that there is no matter, no energy out there; that we create it, materialize it. That's not what is meant. There is a reality, but there are no things, no trees, no birds. These patterns are what we create. As we focus on a particular pattern and then cut it out from the rest, it becomes an object. Different people will do it differently, and different species will do it differently. What we see depends on how we look. This insight happened very dramatically in physics with Heisenberg.

The analogy I have developed is that of the Rorschach test. Imagine a particular type of Rorschach test where you don't have several blots but just one ink blot in which everything interconnects. If I ask you, "What do you see in that part over there?" you might say, "I see a sailboat." Then I ask Thomas. He might say, "I see a squirrel" or something like that. How can he see a squirrel and you, a sailboat? Because the two of you cut out things slightly differently. Then, of course, there's the interpretation and all that. But it's also the cutting out that is different. So the subjectivity in the process of observation is intimately linked with the connectedness of everything. If the world is a network of relationships, then what we call an object depends on how we delineate it, how we distinguish it from the rest of the network. And in this sense we're bringing forth the world.

DAVID: And everything that we order is a reality, you say. But in what sense?

FRITJOF: Basically it's experience! We order our own experience.

DAVID: We want to be careful here. I think that you are trying to stress that what is out there is in itself no more than just material to be experienced.

FRITJOF: Right. And even to say "material" would really be putting it in a category. There is something to be experienced, and different beings experience it differently.

DAVID: Thomas, would there be a parallel on the theological side to this constructivism? One sentence that comes to my mind is a key sentence of Thomistic theology: "Whatever is received is received according to the form of the receiver."

THOMAS: That's a basic principle of knowledge. There's an immanence in all knowing; it's always knowing of the object from within the subject. Perhaps in theology the nearest parallel would be the notion of all knowing as a kind of participation in an ongoing dialogue with reality.

DAVID: And in the context of revelation, it would imply that what we really know about God is always only our experience of God. Whatever we say about God is projection. We can speak with conviction only about our experience of God.

FRITJOF: This would mean then that we create God in our image rather than he creates us in his image.

THOMAS: Not "rather than" but "both."

DAVID: Yes, that it is both is implied in Meister Eckhart's famous line "The eye with which I see God is the very eye with which God sees me." It has often been said that we cannot help imagining God in our own likeness. Even the Greek philosophers said that if the frogs had a god, it would be a divine frog.

FRITJOF: Certainly a lot of what you said about religious experience would fit very well with the constructivist point of view. In science there's a famous saying by Einstein. Einstein said that it was a miracle to him that our abstract mathematical forms would fit reality so neatly that we can describe things we observed outside in terms of things we made up. That to Einstein was just profoundly mysterious.

To Maturana that's not a mystery at all, because for him there is no objective reality, there are only subjective patterns of experience. And all we do is compare different patterns of the experience of the same human being.

DAVID: Even that's not all that new; the Greek definition of a human being as *zōon logikon* is not correctly translated as "rational animal." It means an animal that has the *logos,* or the "word," the principle of reading patterns. The Greek *logos* is the pattern that makes a cosmos out of chaos. We are animals who have that logos within us, and therefore, we can understand the cosmos.

FRITJOF: But we are not the only ones. That holds for all living beings, except that we reflect on it.

DAVID: So here we have to make that important distinction between reflective consciousness and consciousness. Obviously reflective consciousness comes in only with us humans, possibly with higher animals.

FRITJOF: And, you see, in systems theory reflective consciousness comes in with language. To the extent that animals are capable of language, they will have it, too.

The other type of consciousness, which I would rather not call consciousness but awareness, is in all living beings according to the systems view.

DAVID: Would you go further down? Would you consider that something like that awareness could be there all the way down to the subatomic particles?

FRITJOF: No. In this theory, awareness is a dimension of self-organization. Remember when I talked about self-organization, I talked about three dimensions or three aspects—structure, pattern, and process. Mental process, or cognition, as the process of self-organization is characteristic of all life but is not characteristic of nonliving forms.

DAVID: How then does this suddenly spring into existence?

FRITJOF: It doesn't suddenly spring into existence. The roots of mind go deep down into the nonliving world, and aspects of it are present. But it doesn't come together before you have a cell. The cell is the simplest organism we know that has these mental characteristics.

DAVID: At the other end of our scale, we could now probably say that the roots of this reflective consciousness may even be in the animals that use language, not just signals but language, particularly in the higher primates, but those are only the roots. It comes to itself, in human community. That is the important thing. Human community.

Consciousness, purposefulness

FRITJOF: Maybe I should say a few more words here about consciousness. Maturana says that consciousness arises with language. The precursor is communication. He defines communication not as the transmission of a message about an outside reality but rather as the coordination of behavior through continual mutual interaction. It is not yet language; it's sort of a protolanguage. Language arises when you have communication about communication. Here's an example: He says, When I get up in the morning, and my cat comes to the kitchen and meows, and I go to the refrigerator and give her some milk, that's communication. It's a coordination of behavior. If some morning I don't have milk and if the cat were able to say, "Hey, what's the matter? I've meowed three times. Where's the milk?" that would be language. It would be communication about communication. The cat is not able to do that, of course.

Maturana goes on from there to an analysis of language. This communication about communication presupposes a structure of labels that Bateson called logical types. It involves self-reference, the reference to oneself. It also involves the notion of objects, concepts, symbols, and so on. The whole realm of self-awareness and consciousness arises through language. The most radical statement then comes when Maturana says that consciousness is essentially a social phenomenon, because it arises through language that operates in a social system. Not only can we not understand consciousness through physics and chemistry, we cannot even understand it through biology or psychology if we restrict ourselves to a single organism. You will understand consciousness when you go to the social domain.

THOMAS: You could also go to liberation theology; a method that emphasizes the social dimensions of theological knowing would connect with what you are saying.

FRITJOF: Can you say a little more about that?

THOMAS: In liberation theology, the understanding of faith is always a social understanding that takes place at the common grass-roots level among the people who are the believers. Liberation theology stresses that an understanding of Christian faith only makes real sense when it arises out of and speaks to the lived experience of actual communities of people: their needs, their sufferings, their aspirations. A theology that fails to address the plight and disenfranchisement of the poor is pointless and empty.

DAVID: I was asked once by Lex Hixon, who produced an excellent ecumenical program at the Pacifica radio station, WBAI, in New York, to talk about Christianity. My answer was that it seemed ridiculous for one person alone to talk about Christianity. If you really want to convey what Christianity is, it's a communal affair. I suggested they could bring together a whole group of people; we'd sing together, break bread, talk together, so that the audience could somehow get the flavor of community. And they did that! We went on and on; there was no time limit. WBAI aired this program several times because everybody liked it so much. It gave the flavor of Christian community.

I still have a question about the self, though. I was trying to follow you, but you took a quick step. What were you saying about the way we arrive at the notion of the self, Fritjof?

FRITJOF: It begins with objects. The fact that you talk with a communicator about communicating leads you to the notion of an object. From the flow of experience, you abstract and you say, "There's an object." One could go into more steps about how this arises, but that's the first step. Then the notion of the object is applied to one's own person, to the system itself. That leads to the notion of the self as an ego.

DAVID: It is very stimulating to think about the self in this way. But it seems to me a rather roundabout way to get to the notion of the self, sort of from the outside. We need to go to our own experience. The self can be understood in the context of belonging. The self is that to which you belong whether you like it or not.

FRITJOF: But this is not what I mean when I say the self. In this context, I mean the restricted image of the self, which is called the ego. This is very important when we talk about consciousness, because this is how we can abstract ourselves from the true reality in which we live.

DAVID: That self is rather negative then. It is the little self rather than the real self.

FRITJOF: In the same sense that objects also are something negative, but they're something very useful. If I say, "Please give me your pen," it's useful to think of a pen as an object. I could also say there is this pattern of relationships and so on and so forth, but as a shorthand notion, I can say, "May I borrow your pen?"

DAVID: But how then do you protect this little self from thinking it's the real self? It seems sort of harmless, but it is inclined to go wrong, to get stuck, entrapped, and separated. The confusion between the ego and the true self can do a great deal of harm. How do you prevent that?

FRITJOF: I think that brings us back to the beginning of our discussion. There we spoke about belonging, the experience of belonging, and we said that personhood is defined through relationships. But relationship is not something specific to the human. It occurs in all patterns, living and nonliving. What is specifically human is this property of self-awareness. This property of self-awareness has its dangers. It also has its glory. We have magnificent theories, we have culture, art, all of that, but it can also be self-destructive. Therefore it has to be coupled with responsibility, and we have to link the little self to the big self, and that's the *religio*—religion.

DAVID: This places the connection between science and religion in a whole different perspective, doesn't it? The self that typically does science as a scientist is the little self; if it gets separated from the true self, from the sense of belonging to all, it can get dangerous. The alienated little self leads science in a direction that gets us in trouble unless we make the effort of *religio,* take the religious initiative. I like the way you made that clear.

Further reflections on criteria 2 and 3

FRITJOF: Before we go on to the next criterion, I would like to make a comment about criteria 2 and 3. The second criterion in theology is the shift from revelation as timeless truth to revelation as historical manifestation.

DAVID: Yes, from a "package of truth" we shift to revelation as an intrinsically dynamic process. Revelation is the process of coming to know the divine reality through all reality.

FRITJOF: So you focus on the process of knowledge, the process of coming to know the divine reality. Now, in science my third criterion refers to the process of knowledge, whereas my second criterion does not. It refers to processes I observe in nature. So in theology criteria 2 and 3 really seem to flow together.

DAVID: Maybe I can clarify criterion 2 once more, so as to set it off from criterion 3. In the old thinking in theology, all the emphasis was on statements about God, on the teachings, on dogma. Those clearly formulated truths were all that mattered. In the new thinking the emphasis is on the gradual process in which revelation took place. For Christian theology the Bible records the ways human beings gradually came to understand the divine. Revelation history is the process on which theology reflects. Revealed truth corresponds to the structure that is a manifestation of the underlying process, the process of interaction between God and us.

FRITJOF: So the structure would be the doctrine, and the underlying process is the process of the interaction between the human and the divine, how this doctrine came into being. But when you talk about the doctrine, you talk about knowledge.

DAVID: Yes, revelation is a process by which we come to know God; and theology is, too, in its own way. Can you say once more how criteria 2 and 3 differ when we speak about the shift in science?

FRITJOF: Criterion 2 is when I look, for example, at a tree. In the old paradigm I would say the tree consists of certain fundamental structures—the trunk, the branches, the leaves, the roots—and I would describe those as well as I could. Then I would say that they also interact, and then I would describe those processes of interactions, but the structures come first. In the new paradigm I would say the tree is a phenomenon that connects the sky and the earth. It does so with the process of photosynthesis, which takes place in the leaves. For maximum efficiency, the leaves are distributed on the branch in a certain way so they all turn toward the sun. They need to be nourished, and this is why you need a trunk and this is why you need the roots. You have the nourishment from the earth and the nourishment from the sun, and the two mix in the tree. Lots of processes are involved, and those processes create certain structures, and this is what we see when we look at the tree. This is not talking about the process of how I gain knowledge about the tree. It is talking about what the tree is.

Criterion 3 is about the process of knowledge. That's a different level. There when I talk about the tree, I do so only because I observe it; and what is that process of observation? So there are two different processes. The process of gaining knowledge belongs to number 3; the process I observe in nature belongs to number 2. It seems to me that in theology the two flow together.

DAVID: I understand now what you mean. We can clearly distinguish two criteria in theology as well. But here they're closer to one another than they are in science. Thomas, would you please illustrate this distinction with an example from theology? The Trinity, let's say.

THOMAS: I'll try my best. Again, I'll have to use some technical jargon, so please bear with me!

Scientists speak of the relation between "structure" and "process" in reality; theologians speak of the relation between the "immanent" and the "economic" Trinity, or, to use the terms of our criterion 2, between the Trinity as a "timeless truth" and as a "historical manifestation." Let me explain. The Bible and other sources for this doctrine speak about the three divine Persons, Father, Word (or Son), and Spirit, in relation to human salvation, or, in other words, about God as God is toward us. Now, "God toward us" is God revealed through the divine "economy" or plan for humans and the whole cosmos. So the Trinity is "economic" in so far as it impinges upon our lives in the world and in history. But the article of Christian faith states that this "economic" Trinity *is* the "immanent" Trinity, that the God who saves us from our alienation and draws us into a communion of love *is* Father, Word, and Spirit. The process whereby we come to know something of the inner life of God is that same process whereby we are spiritually transformed, liberated, enlightened.

You could push the analogy between the scientific and the theological criterion a little farther and say that the "structure" corresponds to the "immanent Trinity" and the "process" to the "economic Trinity." By being drawn into a dynamic web of relationships with God—the divine "economy"—we come to a paradoxical turn. In science, structure is seen as the manifestation of an underlying process; but theology penetrates beneath the process and discovers the "structure" of God, which is itself a dynamic web of relationships.

DAVID: In other words, we are no longer talking about three Somethings that are sitting out there; we are talking about it in dynamic terms, of how we are imbedded in this reality.

THOMAS: That's precisely it. You know, sometimes Christians forget how the Church came to know about the Trinity of Persons in the one God. They imagine that this doctrine came, as it were, shrink-wrapped direct from heaven. If that were so, then why did the Church need to hold a long series of ecumenical councils in order to hammer out the words to express the inexpressible mystery of God? There are no shrink-wrapped dogmas! The hammering-out of a shared understanding of the mystery is itself a moment in the process of salvation and liberation and enlightenment. The "economic" Trinity, the Trinity that "really matters," because it has to do with our being transcendentally human, simply *is* the Trinity of God, the divine Being's own self-experience. The Trinitarian dogma "really matters" because our groping (as a Church body and as individual believers) toward a clearer understanding of the mystery is in some way the mystery itself. Our struggling to know the Trinity as the Trinity is in God (the "immanent" Trinity) is an integral part of the knowing itself and makes the process of knowing identical with the process of being saved, liberated, enlightened.

DAVID: I wish more people could have the Trinity presented to them in this way! They would realize how our own life partakes of this process of revelation.

FRITJOF: So revelation is a process. Could you say, then, that revelation is a process of gaining knowledge, and theology is gaining knowledge about revelation? So there are two processes of gaining knowledge, two levels.

DAVID: That is the point. In criterion 3 we are dealing with something quite different from criterion 2. In 2 we say that theology is shifting its attention from the product to the process of revelation. Here now, in criterion 3, we note that doing theology is a process that implies our mystic awareness and must explicitly reflect on that epistemic fact.

FRITJOF: So revelation is a process of knowing the divine reality (2), and theology is a process of knowing about revelation (3). In 3 we say our methods of observation and our techniques have to come into the theory; that's why we call it epistemic. The difficulty I had was that revelation itself is a process of knowledge, whereas the photosynthesis in the trees, for example, is not a process of knowledge.

DAVID: And that is why the two criteria are more closely related in theology; but they can still be distinguished.

4 Shift from Building to Network as Metaphor of Knowledge

FRITJOF: Architectural metaphors are frequently used in science to talk about knowledge. We talk about "basic building blocks of matter," "fundamental equations," "fundamental principles," and so on. Knowledge must be built on firm foundations. Then the paradigm shifts occur, shaking the foundations, and everybody gets very nervous. Now we are moving to the metaphor of knowledge as a network rather than a building, a web where everything is interconnected. There is no up and down; there are no hierarchies; nothing is more fundamental than anything else. This shift in metaphors from knowledge as a building to knowledge as a network is my fourth criterion.

DAVID: In theology it's exactly the same. The same architectural metaphors were used all the time in the old paradigm—our basic beliefs, our basic belief structure, and so on.

THOMAS: Even more important than the metaphor was the generally static view of knowledge that it implied. In old-paradigm theology "revealed truth" was a static entity, sent down *en bloc* from heaven. Theological statements were "objective," conveyors of a meaning independent of the believers and their culture. Today the "network" metaphor is starting to prevail in theology. There is a great deal of cross-cultural and interdisciplinary networking, even more than in the physical sciences. Perhaps this is another instance in which theology has advanced more rapidly than science.

FRITJOF: In science this shift is one of the most difficult things to accept, because scientists are so conditioned by the old metaphor. It has become so ingrained in the language of science that it's very difficult now to shift to this "network thinking." For example, most biologists would think that the genetic level of the DNA, the genetic code, and so on is really the basic level that determines everything else. In the new thinking you would say this is one level, one aspect of living systems, but it's not the one on which everything else builds.

Variety of Christian theologies

DAVID: On the theological side there's also a parallel in this respect. It's one of the most difficult things to accept for certain people, particularly for those theologians who have a great stake in having everything neatly nailed down. You hear comments nowadays from old-timers who will say, "We must not allow these many different voices of theologians. We must not allow this great variety of viewpoints because it just confuses the faithful." Behind that stands the idea that in the beginning of Christian theology there was this monolithic, solid, apostolic faith. It sort of stood there at Pentecost, more or less ready-made. All that was necessary was to develop it in more detail. In the course of time different heresies broke away from this original, monolithic faith.

   In reality, however, the picture is quite different. It has been well established by historical research during the past few decades that there was not simply one Christian theology during the first century; there was a great variety of theologies, all of them equally Christian, in spite of being so different from one another. In fact, only through this colorful diversity was it possible to express the full spectrum of the one *lumen Christi,* the light of Christ. That is why the New Testament lets theologies as different as those of Paul and James, of John, Peter, and Luke stand side by side. No attempt is made to homogenize them. They balance and correct one another.

THOMAS: Theologians today admit that historical criticism and the application of its methods to the Bible forced Christian theology to recognize, if only to avoid falling into contradiction, the plurality of theological perspectives in the New Testament. Although no biblical author, not even Saint Paul, builds a complete theological system, you can and must talk about various theologies, in the sense of varying perspectives on the mystery of Christ.

DAVID: All of them shared one common conviction: "Jesus Christ is Lord." "Is that all?" we may wonder. Well, it may indeed be the only common ground shared by all the earliest Christian theologies. A small part of ground, but a patch of bedrock, firm enough to carry the weight of all future theologies. To say "Jesus Christ is Lord" isn't just pious poetry, an enthusiastic acclamation. It is a commitment to measure all public matters by the standard Jesus Christ set by his life and his teachings. Once we have so clear and firm an expression of the core of faith acknowledged by all, we can afford to allow for great diversity in what is less central. Today we are rediscovering Augustine's principle "In essentials unity, in nonessentials freedom, in all things charity." As long as we keep this common bond, the greater the variety of theologies today, the better off we will be.

God as the architect

FRITJOF: I think there is a connection here, not just a parallel but an actual connection, between science and theology. Old-paradigm science believed that there was an ultimate scientific theory about the world, a building with solid foundations. The foundations were the fundamental pieces of matter, the fundamental laws, the fundamental forces in nature, the fundamental equations.

Newton and his contemporaries believed that nature was a book in which we could read the will of God, the way God created the world. So what you really read is God's mind in nature in the sense that God reveals to us the package of truth. As scientists, we do this by observing nature and then deducing from this observation how God created nature and all these fundamental things. In theology you also say there is a fundamental package of truth that was revealed by God. So in the old paradigm God is really the creator of that package both in science and in theology.

THOMAS: Few people know about Newton's theological interests. In fact, he dedicated most of his mature years to biblical research that today we would regard as fruitless, like calculating the date of creation from the ages of the patriarchs in the Book of Genesis.

DAVID: It seems that you don't even have to go back to the time of Newton, because even though the reference to God dropped out of the picture, the picture didn't change.

FRITJOF: No, the picture didn't change. In fact, it's quite interesting that in contemporary science, God has not completely dropped out of the picture. God dropped out of the official texts, so you won't find God in a scientific paper. But you will often find God as a metaphor. One of the most famous examples is Einstein's phrase "God doesn't play dice."

DAVID: Would you assign this to old-paradigm thinking?

FRITJOF: Oh yes, absolutely. This is an old notion of God, a God who is separate from the creation, who sits out there somewhere in the void playing dice and then reaches in according to what the dice show and meddles with the world.

DAVID: Are you saying this is Einstein's notion? He says explicitly, "God does *not* play dice."

FRITJOF: Yes, but he uses that metaphor. He doesn't say that's the wrong notion of God. He argues whether or not God is playing dice. For Einstein, God interferes with the world in a different way, in a way that is much more meaningful, but he is still sitting out there doing something to the world, imposing his will on the world.

That, by the way, is exactly the position of Stephen Hawking. God sits out there and has various options, and Stephen Hawking wonders which option he will take. Hawking is one of the most brilliant scientists today, and his book, *A Brief History of Time,* is brilliant in terms of physics and cosmology, but it is at the level of elementary-school catechism in terms of theology. And it's full of theology! God is in every chapter. Hawking says explicitly, "I want to understand the mind of God."

In the old paradigm where you had the building of knowledge, God is really the architect of the building. The fundamental elements, the fundamental building blocks, are fundamental because God put them in as the architect. We are just discovering them.

In the new paradigm there are things that are fundamental in every scientific model. By definition these fundamental things defy further explanation. But this is only a temporary state of affairs. In the next, more comprehensive model, some of these things will be explained. This means that some of them will be connected to others, will be put into a broader context. But as long as we do science, some things will always remain unexplained.

In a sense, what is fundamental depends on the scientist. It is not objective. In this network thinking, where all concepts and theories are interlinked, you may very well have one theory that has some "fundamental" elements that are explained by another theory. So what is fundamental is a matter of scientific strategy. It depends on the scientist, and it's not permanent.

DAVID: In fact, whether God is mentioned or not really doesn't make a difference here at all. Or does it?

FRITJOF: No, it doesn't. It's just interesting, from a sociological point of view, that God does sneak in.

DAVID: And the fact that God is explicitly mentioned does not necessarily make it old paradigm.

FRITJOF: Not necessarily, but it generally does because God is generally mentioned in the old-paradigm sense, as the creator of the universe in the old-fashioned, fundamentalist sense.

THOMAS: Apparently fundamentalism is a general cultural problem today, involving not only theology but other fields as well.

DAVID: Do you have any idea how one could speak about God or, if you don't want that term, Ultimate Reality, in the new paradigm?

FRITJOF: Yes. For a scientist this would be the horizon of the theory. When I come to the limits of the theory, when I say, "Now, there's so much context, so much interconnectedness that I can not express this in words any more." That would be the area where you could talk about God if you wanted to. But you would not put God as the creator into the scientific theory. People don't do this seriously now, but metaphorically they do.

DAVID: Let me expand on this a little further. How can we speak about God in the new paradigm? The moments of religious encounter are always moments in which something becomes meaningful. In other words, you see something in its ultimate context. We have an idiomatic expression in which we say, "It tells me something" or "It speaks to me." That idea of a dialogue is very strong in the context of finding meaning.

Does it ring true to you—not now as a scientist necessarily but as a human being trying to see things in their ultimate context—to say that through making sense of the world, through understanding this world more deeply, we have the experience of being in contact with that source of it all in the sense that it "tells us something"? It tells us something about itself; it tells us something about ourselves. The model of a dialogue is not completely inapplicable.

FRITJOF: No, it isn't.

DAVID: I'm happy with your answer, because this dialogical dimension of meaning is very strongly my own experience. If you can see that, then we have a new way of introducing God into this picture. Then God is no longer the one who has set this world up in such and such a way, but we have moved to a historical interaction. This is what I called the historical process of revelation, in which we are active partners. There are mystic statements in Western tradition that point toward this understanding. For instance, there is an Islamic statement (I think it's even from the Koran), "I was a hidden treasure and so in order to be found, I created the world."

FRITJOF: In the Hindu myths, there is the concept of *lila,* the "divine play," which is very similar.

THOMAS: This is certainly one of those points where the Mediterranean wisdom tradition coincides with that of India and Asia. In the Book of Proverbs, chapter 8, Wisdom personified is spoken of as a feminine figure, playing alongside God at the moment of creation. Wisdom is at play. Here is another important point: Work is to play as purpose is to meaning; we work to achieve a purpose, but we play to arrive at meaning. Our own knowledge of the meaning of the universe is dependent on our ability to enter into the logic of Wisdom's play. Remember, too, that the Old Testament Wisdom theology is drawn on by the New in elaborating its understanding of the mystery of the Word incarnate in Jesus and of the Spirit—in Hebrew the word *Spirit* is also feminine—poured out upon the disciples at Pentecost.

DAVID: In a Jewish story from Hasidic mysticism, a little boy, the rabbi's grandson, comes crying and says, "I hid myself so well and no one was looking for me." These children were playing hide and seek. The rabbi, tears in his eyes, says, "Oh, now I know what God is saying to me: 'I've hidden myself so well that no one is seeking me.'" So a game is going on, and we are invited to play.

Dialogue with nature

FRITJOF: This relates to something in science that I think is very important. Old-paradigm science, as we discussed before, is motivated by the desire to dominate and control nature. The new paradigm recognizes, first of all, the world as being alive, no longer a mechanical, dead system but a living system, which has its own intelligence, its own "mindfulness," as Bateson said. Therefore the exploration of nature becomes a dialogue. So the metaphor shifts from domination and control to dialogue. Actually this metaphor of dialogue has been used throughout science and also throughout modern science. It is usually referred to as a dialogue with nature. Scientists wouldn't use the term *God* in this context, but the meaning comes close.

DAVID: Theology would simply put this into the ultimate context and say that our dialogue with nature can be understood as dialogue with the deepest source of everything, the divine wellspring. It's in this context that the scientist and the theologian are really joined in one and the same pursuit.

Tolerance and pluralism

FRITJOF: I still have some doubts regarding the issue of different perspectives within science and theology. One of the great proponents of this network-thinking in science is Geoffrey Chew in his bootstrap physics. According to Chew's theory, nature cannot be reduced to any fundamental entities. Physical reality is seen as a dynamic web of interrelated events. Things exist by virtue of their mutually consistent relationships, and all of physics has to follow uniquely from the requirement that its components be consistent with one another. Chew writes in one of his early papers, "Somebody who is able to view different models without prejudice, without saying that one is more fundamental than the other, is automatically a bootstrapper." In other words, this bootstrap, or network philosophy, leads you to an attitude of tolerance.

You say that there have always been several perspectives in theology. Then one of those monopolized Catholic theology and called itself the Catholic tradition. And now in contemporary theology again there are different perspectives. However, the Catholic Church is known as being very intolerant. The pope and the Church hierarchy have often been very intolerant. What is the situation now with regard to pluralism?

THOMAS: The situation is ambiguous, as always. Any honest Church historian will recognize that "theological pluralism" has generally rung the wrong bells in Christendom since Constantine. So you have to distinguish between the sociopolitical intolerance that may prevail, even in the Church, and the fact of a plurality of theological perspectives and emphases. Such a plurality is a fact today, and my impression is that current attempts to rein it in are doomed to be less successful than in the past.

DAVID: Having a monolithic doctrine is of course seen as an advantage by any monarchic power structure.

FRITJOF: An ideology.

DAVID: Yes, that's what an ideology is: doctrine made subservient to power. So theology is always in danger of turning into an ideology through being manipulated by an authoritarian hierarchy. Whenever you have an authoritarian power structure, also in some of the other churches, theology tends to become a tool of power. The Second Vatican Council emphasized a healthy distribution of power in the Church through the collegiality of bishops. Hand in hand with this event, of course, came a pluralism of theological opinions within the Church.

FRITJOF: Where is the pluralism in theology today?

THOMAS: Maybe I could give a general answer. The plurality of perspectives in theology today is the consequence of three sociocultural facts: global communications, which have made it possible for people everywhere to experience their unity-in-diversity with everyone else; the emerging awareness of women, the poor, the oppressed, that they can and must achieve the power—spiritual, economic, political—necessary for their own liberation; and the meeting and dialogue of humanity's religious traditions. The third fact has been visibly promoted by Pope John Paul II; remember the meeting of the religious representatives at Assisi in 1986. And so we see the beginnings of a theology couched in Hindu or Buddhist or African terms. Liberation theology, in spite of some negative statements from the Vatican—not so much from the pope himself as from one or another of his collaborators—continues to flourish and has spread from Latin America to Asia and Africa. All this is taking place within earshot of everyone on the planet.

DAVID: One specific example would be a broader theological spectrum of views concerning the Eucharist. In the old paradigm you have to use one particular set of terms to describe the Eucharist, *transubstantiation* being the key term. But this presupposes a whole construct of philosophy with which many people today are no longer familiar.

The new thinking in theology rejoices in a great variety of ways of speaking about this central mystery of Christian worship. Should we not rejoice that there is such a variety of perspectives and insights as long as they are not in contradiction to the one central belief?

FRITJOF: You mean to what Christ meant, what his message was?

DAVID: Right. The basic meaning that through this particular cultic action, we communicate in a unique way with God through Christ in the Holy Spirit and so with all other human beings and all other creatures. That would be quite central and, stated in that way, it would be acceptable to many different theologies.

FRITJOF: Could you relate this to the sense of belonging?

DAVID: Well, the Eucharist could be understood as a celebration of our ultimate belonging, and as such it has to be all-inclusive. That would, of course, mean that everybody is welcome at the table, because that's what belonging is all about. Understood in this way, the Eucharist would be a celebration of our belonging to the one tradition of Jesus Christ, but it would, by its very symbolism, explode this tradition to include all traditions. It would be a celebration of belonging to the whole of creation, a celebration of our ultimate belonging to God.

FRITJOF: And of course there is nothing more appropriate to celebrate that belonging than a meal, because the ecological cycles are such that we eat each other. This is the cycle of birth and death. The ultimate belonging to an ecosystem is that we are intertwined in these cycles of birth and death, and that's what we celebrate when we celebrate a meal.

DAVID: What you just said is a good example of the way new-paradigm thinking in science can give us a new appreciation of religious realities. Eucharistic theology deals with the mystery of death and life. It is in view of this death that Jesus Christ is giving us his body to eat. There are even references in Christian tradition to the fact that by eating from this bread you become bread for everyone else. This strong communal aspect of the Eucharist is stressed by the new thinking in theology.

But I always have to say that the new thinking in theology is really a return to the oldest thinking. This can not be emphasized too strongly. We are really talking about the oldest, the original, way of thinking about the Christian mysteries. What you call the old paradigm in theology is really not all that old. I wonder whether this is not also true of the new paradigm in science. Pre-science has a history of thousands of years in which people were carrying on a dialogue with nature. I wonder if there isn't a parallel.

FRITJOF: There is definitely a parallel. In a sense we're going back to the preindustrial age, the premodern age. But it's not *just* going back. In new-paradigm science and in the new social paradigm, there are important differences between what we now call the new paradigm and what was happening before the old paradigm.

For instance, there are many parallels between medieval science and new-paradigm science today. There are the holism, the integration, the ecological awareness, but there are also many differences. One difference would be, for instance, the patriarchal modes of expression, the patriarchal order.

DAVID: But the basic approach in medieval science seems to be closer to the new thinking than to, say, nineteenth-century science.

FRITJOF: Yes, in many ways. But, of course, we also build the new-paradigm science on the achievements of the Galilean, Newtonian science. We do science with instruments, with technologies that are built on the Newtonian achievements.

DAVID: Consistency and continuity seem important in theology, too.

THOMAS: I would say that they are essential in theology. Newman, in his classic *Essay on the Development of Doctrine*, used the metaphor of growth from childhood to adulthood. Or you could go back to the words of Jesus: "I have not come to destroy, but to fulfill."

FRITJOF: I would like to come back to the monolithic system in the old paradigm and the pluralism in the new paradigm, both in science and in theology. I think there is a very interesting parallel between the two fields. The monolithic structure in science is forcefully preserved by the scientific advisers to governments who are part administrators, they are part of the power structure, and they are part scientists.

DAVID: Right away I can think of parallels in the Church.

FRITJOF: Right. They're not really scientists, because they don't do science anymore; they sit in Washington and advise the government. They don't do research, and because they don't do research, they're not up on the latest developments, and they forcefully represent old-paradigm science.

DAVID: We, too, have examples of this sort. People who once were quite progressive theologians now sit in power positions in the Vatican, just like your scientific advisers in Washington. I do not think that they have lost contact with theological developments. In our case, it's more a matter of pastoral concern. I will give them credit for that. They fear that the faithful will become confused if we allow pluralism in theology. What appears to conservatives as contradictory is merely a variety of perspectives on one and the same reality.

FRITJOF: The crux here is that you say we're talking about perspectives on the same *reality*. Old-paradigm theology was not even concerned with the reality, only with the teaching. If you take the teaching as the reality, then there can't be perspectives.

DAVID: There's some truth to that. And variety of perspectives is necessary also for pastoral reasons. By allowing variety of perspectives, we are making genuine understanding available to a great variety of people. When we cut Christian doctrine down to only one version, we are cutting out all those people for whom this version is not acceptable, but to whom another equally valid version would speak.

THOMAS: The basic problem in official Catholic theology has always been the tendency to confuse doctrinal integrity with the integrity of faith. Of course, no theologian in his right mind would say that the doctrine as formulated in words and concepts is the object of faith; only God is. But the fear of error has sometimes made theologians cling to the formulas in a way that verges on idolatry.

5 Shift from Truth to Approximate Descriptions

Approximation in science

FRITJOF: In science the fact that we recognize that our statements are limited and approximate is very much linked to the recognition that we are dealing with a network of relationships we ourselves are a part of. But if everything is connected to everything else, how can you ever explain anything? Explanation, as we said before, is showing how things are connected to other things. If everything is connected to everything, you can not explain anything, right?

The properties of any part arise from the way they are related to the properties of the other parts. You can never hope to explain the property of any part unless you accept approximate explanations. Approximate explanations mean that you are taking into consideration some of the interconnections but not all. You make progress by including more and more, but you will never get the complete picture. For example, in Newtonian mechanics the resistance of air is generally not taken into account. In particle physics the effects of gravity are generally neglected, and so on. That's the scientific method; we go from approximative model to approximative model, and we improve the approximation.

THOMAS: The manualistic paradigm of theology suggested by its very form as "summa" or compendium that our theological knowledge was exhaustive. The new paradigm, by greater emphasis on mystery, acknowledges the limited and approximate character of every theological statement. Theology can never provide a complete and definitive understanding of the divine mysteries. The theologian, like every believer, finds ultimate truth not in the theological statement but in the reality to which this statement gives a certain true but limited expression.

Dogma

FRITJOF: At this point it might be appropriate to discuss the notion of dogma, which has played such an important role in the history of Catholic theology. What is dogma?

DAVID: I would say, in the theological enterprise, sometimes you come across very important points that are being questioned. Dogma is almost always a response. It starts with a dispute about some point that is so important that the whole model depends on it. Therefore a great deal of effort is expended on settling that question. In the end a dogmatic decision settles the dispute.

But dogma is a statement *about* reality; it never reaches the reality that lies behind the dogma; it is only approximate. We tend to forget that. The decisive thing about a dogma is that you can say, "This particular point of doctrine has been examined and pinned down, defined.

Let's not waste our energy. This one has been settled." Take, for instance, the doctrine that humanity and divinity are united in Jesus, not mixed. By settling disputes in this way, dogma can be a great help. It frees our energy and becomes a stepping stone for further exploration. I like to borrow Christopher Fry's term and think of theology as "exploration into God," from stepping stone to stepping stone.

FRITJOF: Science has these stepping stones, too. But what is so important in our new understanding of science is that any of these are up for revision at any time. There is no permanent truth, and there is no absolute truth, in the sense of an identity between the description and the thing described.

But the popular meaning of dogma is something you have to accept as the truth, not as just a model.

THOMAS: Dogma in this popular sense implies an act of will. "You have to accept the dogma. You don't have to understand it, you just have to accept it. And you can't question it." I think this way of understanding the term *dogma* is detrimental to a genuinely religious use of dogma. It also renders impossible the *development* of dogma.

FRITJOF: Of course, it is not by accident that this is the popular understanding of dogma. We all know that the Church has insisted on this for centuries.

DAVID: Still today, either you accept a particular dogmatic statement as it stands or you have to bear dire consequences.

FRITJOF: In the past you were burned at the stake. What is the history of the term? Was there a use of *dogma* in the sense that you two are using it in early times? And did that then rigidify? Or is this a new way of seeing it?

THOMAS: I think both ways have always been there. The decision-making process that defined dogmas—the gatherings of bishops called general or ecumenical councils of the Church—began in the fourth century, during the reign of Constantine. At that time Christianity was legalized and eventually became the official religion of the Roman Empire. So there is a sociopolitical aspect in the development of dogma.

In other words, if you're going to belong to the Christian Empire, you're going to have to conform not only to certain ways of behaving but also to certain ways of thinking. At the same time, the great thinkers of the Church were concerned mainly with what dogma meant for the spiritual growth of the person and of the community. The purpose of dogmas, they say, is to guarantee that you will continue your spiritual growth and arrive at a deep personal experience of the mystery that the dogma only approximately expresses.

Let me add a footnote on the root of the words *dogma* and *orthodoxy.* They come from the Greek verb *dokein,* which means "to seem," or "to be recognized," "to have a reputation." So dogma originally meant "opinion," especially the opinion I have of a person, as in the expression "I have a high opinion of you." This is the positive sense of opinion. "Intellectual opinion" is a second meaning; and the third meaning is "an official teaching," the teaching or dogma of a philosophical school, the dogma, finally, of a church.

What was equally important for early Christianity was the other noun derived from the verb *dokein,* which is *doxa,* meaning "glory," the manifestation to me of the qualities of a person. I form my opinion on the basis of the *doxa,* on the basis of the glory of that person. So orthodoxy means the right way of glorifying God, who manifests himself to us, and also the right perception of the glory that emanates from God. Dogma is our glorification of God and of the glory, the *doxa,* that emanates from God.

DAVID: For us today it is necessary to set this into the right perspective. For us glory tends to suggest merely pomp and circumstance of some patriarchal, hierarchical God enthroned on high. We have to go back to the time before this misconception crept in. When Greek was still the official language of the Church, we got this answer to the question, What *is* the glory of God? "The glory of God is the human being fully alive." This statement by St. Irenaeus is one of the earliest theological statements.

THOMAS: The glory of God, then, is closer to the sense of "What a glorious sunset!" That luminosity which illuminates the whole landscape, ourselves included.

DAVID: Fritjof, you asked whether our presentation of dogma is new or traditional. The answer must be that it is both. Unfortunately there were at all times, and there still are today, people who hold a very narrow view of dogma; they identify a dogmatic statement about the truth with the truth about which the statement is made. But there have been others throughout the history of Christian tradition who did not share this narrow understanding of dogma. An example would be Saint Thomas Aquinas. He understood that faith refers to the reality about which the dogmatic statement is made, not to the statement in its particular wording.

THOMAS: You don't make an act of faith in a statement; you don't make an act of faith in a dogmatic definition. You make an act of faith in the reality.

FRITJOF: Well, at this point it may be useful to compare this with the Buddhist tradition. The Buddha, as you know, put forth the Four Noble Truths. And the way I see it, this is the Buddha saying, "Look, you're not happy with the way you are. I can make four statements about your inner life that will be helpful. I can guarantee you that if you act according to those statements—life is suffering; it comes from clinging; the situation has a remedy; and I'll give you the remedy (the Eightfold Path)—you will overcome your problems."

Now, if somebody tells me this, he is not making a statement about the world. You see, the problem in Christianity is that you are asked to believe that the world is such and such, and God is that person, and so on. This sort of challenges you, because it makes a statement about your existence and about the existence of the world. The Buddha says something very different. The Buddha says, "You come to me because you're in trouble, and I have a solution for your troubles," like a doctor almost, or a psychotherapist. "And if you don't want it, fine with me. But if you do, and you're sincere about it, I can help you." That's how I see the Four Noble Truths. Now how does this sound to Christian ears?

DAVID: Well, first, the Four Noble Truths simply express basic human reality. "That's the way it is," the Buddha says. Therefore his message must be acceptable to every human being. We are dealing with facts. The basic message of Jesus is actually of the same kind. It appeals to universal human experience. It can be truly appreciated, understood, and affirmed only when it becomes a person's own experience. In contrast to the teachings of Buddha, however, the Christian message is often mistaken for some kind of immutable truth independent of experience.

FRITJOF: But these Buddhist noble truths are not dogmas in the nar-row sense.

DAVID: Of course not. Yet the facts, as stated by the Buddha, are beyond dispute.

FRITJOF: You're not forced to believe them. Nobody says you have to. It says if you want to try this, here's a remedy.

DAVID: The reason for there not being dogmas in Buddhism lies prob-ably way beyond both Buddhism and Christianity in the context out of which the two traditions grow. Buddhism is basically "apophatic." It insists that you can't say anything about that ultimate reality you encounter in your best moments. Ultimately that experience is unspeakable. Buddhism is a relatively late expression of this apophatic attitude, which is more widespread in the East than in the West.

The Christian tradition grows out of a cataphatic context, where you *can* say something, where you have to say it. Both are anchored in our experience. In our best moments, when we have our religious insights, we know you can't ever put these insights into words, and yet we never cease trying to express them. The Christian tradition comes out of that effort and therefore ends up in dogma sooner or later. A dogma is an insight we have pinned down now, always remembering that its expression is only approximate. In Buddhism, on the other hand, you ultimately end up in silence. Therefore you have the silence of the Buddha. The ultimate teaching of the Buddha is not handed on by words but by the silence of the Buddha.

THOMAS: Of course it is useful to characterize these two approaches in terms of their respective preference for apophatic or cataphatic discourse. But I think that both Christianity and Buddhism remind us that when all is said and done, the mystery is beyond our reach, incomprehensible.

DAVID: Let me ask you something here, Fritjof. Have you had firsthand experience with dogmatism in science?

FRITJOF: Yes, very often.

DAVID: I think there are many examples of that.

FRITJOF: Yes, and the word *dogma* is also used. For instance, there's the Darwinian dogma or the neo-Darwinian dogma.

DAVID: Is there a positive notion to dogma in science?

FRITJOF: No. It's always negative. Let me just tell you what the general situation is. Let's say I have a discussion with a scientist today, any scientist who is a valued, bona fide scientist, sitting across from me like you are now, and I asked, "Is there any absolute statement in science that is true for all times, or are all of these statements limited and approximate?" At least after a short discussion, but probably right away, every scientist would agree that science makes only approximate statements. Everything in science is limited and approximate.

However, in their practical work, scientists very often act as if there were absolute truths, in the sense that those are the things they never question. They would not accept a paper, or would be reluctant to accept a paper, that questioned these dogmas. But when you actually confront them and ask in an abstract, general way whether there is anything really absolute in science, they say no.

DAVID: That is probably how dogmatism comes about: by refusing to question. You would know an answer if you confront the question. But why do you refuse to raise the question? Because of peer pressure? Because it's easier just to go along?

FRITJOF: Not only that. In order to do science, you need a certain framework, and you want to work within this framework. If you questioned everything all the time, you wouldn't be able to do science. But if you never question anything, you won't make progress. Ideally you should pursue a scientific activity within a certain framework, but you should be ready to question any part of that framework at any time.

DAVID: That is then your explanation for how this dogmatism comes about—by not questioning when you ought to question. And how can it be avoided? By being ready to question when you ought to question.

FRITJOF: I have another question. Is there an intent to improve the approximation in theology? This is really characteristic of science. There is scientific progress. There are also, as Thomas Kuhn has described, scientific revolutions where almost everything may be thrown overboard.

DAVID: In order to improve?

FRITJOF: Of course, in order to improve the approximation. So there is gradual improvement and then there is revolutionary improvement, but both are improvements of the approximation.

DAVID: In theology both the old thinking and the new thinking would acknowledge that there is gradual improvement. Improved approximation is the goal. There is gradual progress and improvement in theology as well as in science. But the old thinking would assume that all that has to be said is already there; it just needs to be spelled out more precisely. In the new thinking, theology is an exploration into God; we may come to see the same truth from exciting new perspectives.

That is where dogma comes in handy: certain insights have been pinned down. We can say, "That much of our territory has been mapped out. We don't have to go over this ground again. That much we have already seen. Let's move on."

However, the dogma—and that is its problem—is always expressed in the language of a particular time. Along with the essential point, a dogma may mention things that were not in question, that were not meant to be pinned down. So you have to go back and ask, "What does this really mean in its context? What does its language mean? Why did they stress this point? Why was it so important to them?" This is hard work for theologians. The content of the dogmas does not change, but our understanding of them must again and again be revised.

Progress in science, art, and theology

FRITJOF: But is there an improvement? Is there progress? In science there is progress; you move to ever more comprehensive, precise, and powerful theories—powerful in the sense of predictive power. This is very characteristic of science, and let me contrast this for a moment with art. This is clearly not present in art. You can not say that Picasso is an improvement on Rubens. Or Chagall is an improvement on some classical painter. It would be ridiculous to say that.

DAVID: Not in the sense in which you can say that Einstein is an improvement on Newton, but in another sense I would try to say that there is an improvement in art. There is progress in the sense that a masterwork gives us a new insight into human experience. Something that was not accessible to our experience before Bach or Stravinsky wrote their music is now available for us: a new, a deeper self-understanding, a new vision of reality.

FRITJOF: But is the old one included? Implied in the notion of progress is that the old perspective is included plus something new. Newtonian physics is included in Einstein. Mathematically you can derive Newtonian physics from Einsteinian physics. But you can not derive Michelangelo from Picasso.

DAVID: Picasso from Michelangelo though. I suppose that's what you meant.

FRITJOF: No, I meant derive in the sense that you can see that Newton is included in Einstein. Einstein goes beyond but includes Newton.

DAVID: But you can see in Picasso's work that he presupposes Michelangelo and goes beyond him. In poetry it's the same. In music, too. I think it is not progress in the same sense as in science, but it is a form of progress. The way theology develops might resemble the arts.

THOMAS: I think it does. Like theologians in their reflection on dogma, all artists are aware of the debt they owe to history, of how creativity is impossible without memory, of how illusory the idea of "originality" is. At the same time, history can be a burden. Picasso looked at the millennia of European art history, from the caverns at Altamira to his own day, and felt the weight of it all. In general, theology and the arts are more closely linked than people suppose. Liturgy is art, and it is also, as Pope Pius XI said, the primary medium of the ordinary magisterium or "teaching mission" of the Church. Liturgical art, too, is or can be theology. Think of the icons of the Byzantine tradition or of the mosaics of a great basilica, like Saint Mary Major's in Rome. What theology that is!

DAVID: I think that progress in theology would consist in tracing divine revelation in the events of a particular period in history. In other words, what is God revealing to us in our time through the things that happen? That refers not only to historical events but also to the insights of a given period. Theology speaks of religious reality in terms that are relevant to our experience here and now. That comes pretty close to what an artist does or a poet or a playwright.

FRITJOF: In science it's quite clear that when you have, say, two bodies in relative motion, and you can describe them in terms of Newton's physics and in terms of Einstein's physics, Einstein's physics is the more accurate. You will have a more accurate match of the description and the phenomenon described. In that sense we can say that science has progressed from Newton to Einstein.

DAVID: There is, of course, progress through new information in theology, too. For instance, we have the discovery of the Dead Sea Scrolls, Bible manuscripts that are much older than the earliest manuscripts we had until that time. In 1945 a whole library of Gnostic writings was discovered in Upper Egypt. Through excavations a lot of archaeological material has come to light in our time. The various ways scholars have approached Scripture in recent decades have given us completely new insights into what kind of a library the New Testament is. For it is not one book, as one formerly more or less tacitly assumed; it is a whole library of books that express many different points of view. So we come to compare these points of view.

FRITJOF: That's progress like in science.

DAVID: Yes, to the extent that theology is a science, there is progress.

THOMAS: But, of course, there is a sense in which theology is not a science, and in that sense there is no progress. In any case, we can call progress a myth of our times, taking "myth" for once in the negative sense, as a story that obfuscates our perception of reality.

FRITJOF: When you talked about dogmas, you said that certain dogmas express the truth for the people of a certain epoch, of a certain culture. Suppose you just did a study of an entire doctrine and all its dogmas. You would not need now to go back to something they formulated way back except for historical interest, but you could do it in a contemporary formulation. The whole doctrine could have a contemporary formulation, and you would say that in the future you will expect a different formulation. Again, there would be no need to go back to our time, except for historical interest.

DAVID: No, there is more to it than just historical interest, because those are landmark insights. Like science, theology also affirms certain basic insights, insights upon which later generations will always build. We refer back to these insights, but not necessarily in exactly the same terminology, because language changes. Historic study is always necessary to see the context in which these statements were made. But I think there's a lot of that going on in science, too.

FRITJOF: Yes, I think this is quite parallel.

THOMAS: Historians have played a decisive role in the two new paradigms we're talking about. Think, for instance, of Thomas Kuhn's book *The Structure of Scientific Revolutions* and its impact on the elaboration of the new paradigm in physics, the life sciences, even psychology. In theology Father M. D. Chenu's insistence on the need to reread Aquinas and other theological classics in their historical context caused his work to be put on the Index of forbidden books, but in the end he was invited to the Second Vatican Council as an official expert. The work of a Lutheran historian of theology, Jaroslav Pelikan, is currently having an enormous impact on Catholic theology; his volumes are standard reading in most seminaries today.

DAVID: A while ago, Fritjof, you spoke about the problem of explaining things when they all hang together. If everything hangs together with everything, where do you start? I think theology is not trying to explain in the sense that science explains.

It's more like what you do with a play, say, with *King Lear.* Here you are presented with a little universe where everything hangs together with everything. Here the fullness of life with all its joys and all its sorrows is presented to you in three hours on one stage. When you see this play, you do not have the urge to explain it. You may like to analyze it in terms of literary criticism, but ultimately what really satisfies about it is that you say, "Yes, that's the only way life is." You say yes not to this or that character, not to this or that part of the plot. Somehow you say yes to the underlying reality in the overall microcosm of life presented through this play. That is what great art invites you to do, to say yes to life in its fullness.

FRITJOF: The tragedy of a Shakespeare play is as valid today as it was in Shakespeare's time. He pinpointed something in the human condition that speaks to us as powerfully now as it did then.

Then there are other elements of the human condition that change. If you have a play by Sartre, for instance, like *No Exit,* you could say that this did not exist in Shakespeare's time. This existential angst is a sign of the modern times. It is an alienation characteristic of the modern times that did not exist then. This is a reflection on the social and cultural context of the human condition, which has changed.

DAVID: You wouldn't call that progress.

FRITJOF: Exactly. You wouldn't call it progress.

DAVID: In theology one quite obvious parallel would be in medical ethics, as an aspect of moral theology. Many things are possible in medicine now that just weren't possible before. This introduces new moral questions. On the basis of our relatedness to ultimate values, moral theologians must try to outline appropriate responses in these new areas.

Poetry and literary criticism

FRITJOF: And would you say that there are parts, like in the Shakespeare plays—say, the meeting of Romeo and Juliet, this extremely moving, tender dialogue—parts on which you can't improve? In modern language, there's no improvement. Shakespeare said it all. I suppose you can also say this about certain statements in theology.

DAVID: Indeed. Maybe in theology we call these parts dogmas. You can't improve on them, provided that you speak that language. You have to speak Shakespearean English or else you can't understand those passages in *Romeo and Juliet*. The further our language moves away from Shakespeare's, the more difficult it will become to understand those passages; even though you can't improve on them. Similarly the further our language moves away from the language in which the early Church formulated its dogma, the more we'll have to struggle to surmount the language barrier that separates us from that which cannot be improved upon. It becomes more and more urgent to express it in our own terms.

FRITJOF: But the dogmas are not formulated in poetic language, are they?

DAVID: No, they aren't, and that is part of the problem.

FRITJOF: If they were, people would see it much easier.

DAVID: Right. This points to another great problem: Many of the things that eventually got pinned down in philosophical language as dogmatic formulations were originally poetic statements. As poetry they were much richer and fuller than they were allowed to be when they were forced into the philosophical language of dogmas. Many concepts that ended up in dogmatic formulations have their roots in hymns that the early Christians sang. They were poetry. Religious language is the language of poetry. The language of theology is not poetry; it's the language of philosophy. You could almost say that religious experience expresses itself in poetry, and theology is its literary criticism. (Literary critics have a tendency to take themselves more seriously than their subject and to take the life out of literature.)

FRITJOF: So if you had the dogmas expressed in poetry and continually or from time to time reexpressed in different kinds of poetry, and if you had a theology of literary criticism that pulled all these together, that would be more satisfactory.

DAVID: Possibly so. Actually, what is expressed in philosophical language in the dogmas is available in hundreds of different forms of poetic expression anyway in the rest of tradition.

THOMAS: Let me add a historical footnote here. The great trinitarian and christological dogmas were never totally reduced to "philosophical language," because they were rooted in the language of the Bible. "Dogma" itself may not be a poetic literary genre, but neither is it purely utilitarian language. There is metaphor and allusion in the classical dogmatic definitions, and hence some elements of poetry or poetic prose, as when the Nicene Creed calls the Son "light from light." However, the language of theology does tend to become more arid and sterile as it moves away from the great Patristic and Scholastic epochs into the period we have identified in these conversations as old paradigm, the epoch of Positive-Scholastic or manualistic theology.

DAVID: When we were talking about plays a little while ago, I had another question. Can you compare the poetic universe that's presented to us in a great play with the universe that science presents to us? Could we then compare the meaning of the play, which one finds in each part, but only in view of the whole, with the meaning of the cosmos, which we find only in the ultimate context?

FRITJOF: Yes, absolutely. I think Bateson emphasized this. Bateson emphasized stories, and he defined a story as a pattern of relationships. What is important in a story, what is true in it, said Bateson, is not the people in it or the things or the plot but the relationships between the people. If you follow a story, you follow certain relationships, and you never get the whole meaning, because you don't see the whole as you follow it. After you have read it, you get the meaning, and sometimes even that is not enough. In the Greek dramas, for example, in the Oedipus trilogy, you don't even get it in one play. You need all three plays to see how the act of one person is karmically connected through generations. That's the essence of the Greek tragedy.

DAVID: That seems to me a very apt analogy. Science is concerned with the working of the cosmos. Religion is concerned with the meaning behind it.

THOMAS: Christianity, of course, is also concerned with the meaning behind history, as are Judaism and Islam. These religions are often called prophetic as opposed to the sapiential or mystical religions like Hinduism and Buddhism. But this is too rigid a classification. Buddhism certainly gives meaning to history, in so far as it has an eschatology and proclaims a hope in a future, final Buddha, Maitreya. All religions today are faced with the challenge of history; it is unavoidable. Christians can not claim to have all the answers when it comes to the meaning of our times, although Christianity's theology of history can and does serve as a stimulus to reflection among people of other faiths.

The human element

FRITJOF: We have spoken of theology as a reflection on the exploration into God and of the religious experience as an experience of belonging. It seems to me that whatever you say in theology refers to this experience of belonging. Therefore you are always explicitly in the picture. All theological statements seem to be about a relationship between you and reality.

In science that's not the case, although it is implicitly the case because you cannot separate the observer from the observed phenomena. But you don't talk about the observer explicitly. When I say an atom is made of a nucleus and electrons, and so on, I don't talk about my relationship to the atom. Or when I talk about an ecosystem, and I say that in the forest the squirrels and the trees and the roots and the fungi all work together and interact and there are certain natural cycles, I don't say explicitly that I belong to those cycles.

The religious experience of an ecosystem and the reflection on that religious experience would be different, it seems to me.

DAVID: Definitely so. The awareness of ultimate belonging will always be central to our religious experience. It need not be made explicit, however, in the theological reflection on that experience.

It would be a mistake to assume that theological reflection is concerned with the inner experience while science reflects on the outer. No, both science and theology are concerned with reality as a whole. But theology looks at reality under the aspect of our relationship to God, the Horizon, while science narrows its focus to what is contained within our horizon.

Reality, as I use the term here, comprises both the cosmos and history. That's the vast field of exploration for both science and theology.

FRITJOF: That's where they overlap.

DAVID: Yes, that's where they must find this common ground. In this context I would not want to put undue stress on the personal element in theology. We must also stress that theology as well as science aims at an objective assessment of reality, the best approximation of the truth of the universe, ultimately unfathomable, as it is.

FRITJOF: Let me give you an example. When I wrote *The Tao of Physics,* I juxtaposed quotations from Eastern mystics and from physicists. For instance, I remember a passage in an early Buddhist text, *The Awakening of Faith* by Ashvagosha, that says, "When the mind is disturbed, the multiplicity of things arises. When the mind is quieted, the multiplicity of things disappears." Then he would go on to talk about the fact that there are no fundamentally isolated or separate objects in the world, that this perception is an illusion. This is very close to what physicists have found out in the twentieth century. But Ashvagosha's sentence begins "When the mind is disturbed, . . . " speaking explicitly of the human condition. But other passages of the same text make no mention of the human condition. He talks about gross matter and fine matter and this and that, and these are the statements that I would compare to the statements of physicists.

With theology being related to God in its very name, my feeling from our conversation has been that the relationship to God as personal is really primary. The experience of belonging to the relationship.

DAVID: Yes, it is always primary, but not always explicit, not always in focus. We deal with reality under different aspects. How about yourself, Fritjof? As a physicist, you deal with reality in a scientific way. But you have other ways of dealing with reality on a spiritual level as a religious person. How would you describe the difference between the two attitudes you take when you are wearing those two different hats?

FRITJOF: Well, let's take the experience of reality as an interconnected web and of our being an inseparable part of that web. It would be an intellectual challenge for me, as a scientist, to say something about a phenomenon of which I am part. When I am part of the phenomenon, a kind of self-reference is introduced that makes the whole thing very complicated and messy. To untangle that messiness is a formidable intellectual challenge. In science we work with approximate statements and models. We say that at this level of approximation, I don't have to talk about myself. Since I don't talk about myself at this level, I know I'm making an error, and then I'll try to quantify that error. This is the intellectual, or, as you would say, the noetic, problem.

DAVID: But you also realize then that your clean concept, your clean observation, is impoverished in that it artificially abstracts from the complicated truth of your being caught in a web of interconnections.

FRITJOF: Yes. I would call it approximate. What you call impoverished is exactly the notion of approximation.

DAVID: I'm not sure that I understand you here. When I speak of approximation, I mean that we approach the goal more or less closely. But if we choose only one limited aspect as our goal . . .

FRITJOF: That is impoverished. Impoverished is not having the whole.

DAVID: That's right. Now, the particular aspect of impoverishment that I had in mind just now was this: your personal response to reality has been cut out.

FRITJOF: Yes, I was going to come to that. You asked me how I would see this as a scientist and as a human being. To make the comparison easier, let's talk about the concrete example of an ecosystem, say a forest. As a scientist, I will describe the forest, and I will see that my process of observation is part of the description. That's the messy part. But then if I step out and walk into the forest and really feel emotionally, aesthetically, and spiritually connected to the forest and have a full-blown experience of this kind, it's an existential, spiritual experience. In this case the level that is most important to the scientific description—the intellectual—wouldn't be there at all.

DAVID: Intellectual objectivity could be sacrilegious at that moment.

FRITJOF: The intellectual, reflective, analyzing level is transcended. I wouldn't analyze the experience.

DAVID: This is an important point. Would you say that the intellectual aspect has something to do with getting things into one's grip?

FRITJOF: Absolutely.

DAVID: And the other attitude that you described has something to do with giving ourselves over to the experience; with allowing it to do something to us. This is where the human response comes in; and without that human element nothing has any meaning for us. As a scientist, you are not concerned with the God-question; but as a human being you can not escape its challenge. It is as inseparable from reality as the horizon is inseparable from the landscape.

THOMAS: It seems to me that you have hit upon the point where the new paradigms in science and theology converge: the realization that the "objective viewpoint" is illusory, that in the face of total reality, no one can be a "detached observer." There is a medieval axiom for this, as we mentioned earlier: *Quidquid recipitur, ad modum recipientis recipitur,* "Whatever is received, is received according to the manner of the receiver." The pretense of an objective stance, as you said, David, is sacrilegious. *Tua res agitur!* "It is your story that is being told, you are part of it all." So the shift from the part to the whole also involves the realization that I belong to the whole universe, not as if I were a negligible phenomenon on a small planet in a minor solar system but as a vital participant in the living cosmos. This realization is both the context and the condition of God's self-disclosure.

Social Implications
of New-Paradigm Thinking
in Science and Theology

FRITJOF: The social implications of new-paradigm thinking in science are quite clear to me. Every scientific field that has social relevance, such as medicine, economics, psychology, biology, is needed now to solve society's grave problems, and only a new-paradigm kind of science will be able to solve them. For instance, in medicine, only when the mind and the body are seen as two facets of the same phenomenon will we be able to understand many of today's major illnesses. Only when we see the organism imbedded in society and in the natural ecosystems will we be able to deal with health in a meaningful way. Similarly in economics only if we see the economy imbedded in ecosystems, only if we see the interaction between economic processes and social processes, will we be able to solve the economic crisis.

So it is quite clear that new-paradigm thinking in science has many social implications.

THOMAS: This is also true of the new-paradigm thinking in theology. Our society is rapidly becoming aware that its problems have spiritual implications. Theology, in turn, is becoming aware that answers to these problems can no longer be handed down from above. They must be developed in dialogue with grass-roots movements in society and with the insights of the poor and oppressed. And dialogue is a typically new-paradigm stance in theology.

Interconnectedness and sustainability

FRITJOF: The most crucial implications of new-paradigm thinking for politics today, and for society at large, concern the notion of interconnectedness, which is at the very heart of the new paradigm, this sense of belonging, which we understand as the heart of religious experience. One way interconnectedness comes into the picture in politics is to recognize the interconnectedness of problems. The major problems of our time can not be understood in isolation. Whatever the problem is— environmental destruction, population growth, the persistence of poverty and hunger throughout the world, the threat of nuclear war, to name a few—it has to be perceived as being connected to the others. In order to solve any single problem, we need systemic thinking, because these are all systemic problems, interconnected and interdependent. This is one aspect of the profound implications of new-paradigm thinking in society and in politics.

THOMAS: Are you thinking of another one, Fritjof?

FRITJOF: Yes, there is another kind of interconnectedness, and that is connectedness to the future. Most of our so-called solutions today are solutions that create new problems. For instance, to solve the energy problem with nuclear power may be all right for a time, but it is definitely not all right in the long run, because of nuclear waste and various other problems. Since there is no acceptable storage place for nuclear waste, we will always be left with it. The more we accumulate, the more danger we have in our midst, and the more we have to guard it. So the technical problem of storing radioactive waste turns into the social problem of having to create a police state to guard it. This to me is the strongest argument against nuclear power: it is socially unacceptable because it conflicts with democracy. Nuclear power is inherently undemocratic in the long run.

The viable solutions are those that do not create other problems in the future. To use the term that has become a key term in the environmental movement, the only solutions that are acceptable are *sustainable* solutions. This concept of sustainability was defined by Lester Brown at the Worldwatch Institute: "A sustainable society is one that satisfies its needs without diminishing the prospects of future generations."

DAVID: That's a very simple and very beautiful definition. It's very much in accordance with a traditional Native American position of keeping the seventh generation in mind for all important decisions.

FRITJOF: Sustainability has emerged as a key criterion for deciding about the structure of society that we want to build, and to me the challenge of the 1990s will be to create sustainable societies. Only sustainable societies can resolve the problems that are threatening to destroy us.

The main point I want to make here is that these two issues—the interconnectedness of problems and looking ahead and being responsible to future generations—are pivotal in new-paradigm thinking as far as politics and society are concerned. I was wondering whether theology has a parallel. I know from my own experience of old-paradigm theology that the emphasis is really on eternity and the afterlife, not on future generations. You can say the same about society in general.

THOMAS: There are two perspectives on the situation of human beings in history, which are found at the very beginning of Christianity in the New Testament and which remain in constant tension. One could be called the eschatological emphasis.

FRITJOF: What does that mean, eschatological?

THOMAS: Eschatological, from the Greek word *eschaton* (the last), refers to the presence of the ultimate, the definitive, the final manifestation of God in the present moment, and our focus upon that.

The other perspective, which is represented largely in the Gospel according to Luke and the Acts of the Apostles, sees our historical situation as being in a "middle time" between the beginning time of the Kingdom with Jesus, and the end time, the consummation of the Kingdom. In this middle time, we're responsible for the Kingdom of God. The Kingdom of God is constituted on earth not only in the Church as a religious institution but also in the extension of the fruits of the Kingdom to all human beings.

DAVID: The old-paradigm approach, which is preoccupied with eternity and lasting things, sees only the first of the twofold possibility of emphases that was there from the beginning of Christianity.

THOMAS: The other emphasis sees the unfolding of God's Kingdom as a historical reality, in the sense that it is worked out by human beings in the ongoing process of living in time.

FRITJOF: I think there's a difference to new-paradigm thinking in society, though, and this is a twentieth-century addition. In our general collective awareness there is now a strong sense of the deterioration of the environment. I don't think anybody entertained this notion very widely in the past.

DAVID: But the attitude expressed in the Gospel according to Luke and in Acts can deal with this problem in our time.

THOMAS: It's a resource to be drawn upon even though it has never been rendered explicit in connection with the environment until our own time.

DAVID: And now it must be made explicit. Our time calls for it. And it is no coincidence that Luke and Acts offer the strand of New Testament theology that is most occupied with the poor, with our responsibility for the oppressed, and for setting things right in the world socially.

FRITJOF: To me the closest concept to sustainability I can think of in spiritual traditions is the concept of karma. I can imagine a traditional Buddhist or Hindu telling us, even five hundred years ago, that if we dump toxic waste, this is bad karma. This means that eventually it will come back to us. Karma, of course, implies time only in the context of "future lives," but our children, in a sense, are our future lives. Future generations are our future lives. So karma to me is a very ecological concept.

THOMAS: Every religion today must rediscover its own ecological concepts. The task that the religions of humanity now face is that of drawing on their particular sources and deepest insights in order to modify human behavior, so that our presence on earth will once more be life giving.

DAVID: Right. I remember, for instance, a question a young Jewish student asked his rabbi: Is nuclear power kosher? The rabbi's answer was emphatically "No." This is important, because it sets this problem of our time squarely in the context of Jewish tradition and terminology. In every religious tradition, we will have to face these contemporary problems.

I am also reminded of an important passage in the New Testament in which the new attitude ushered in by John the Baptist is seen as a fulfillment of the prophecy in the Book of Malachi: "He will turn the hearts of the fathers to their children." This has always puzzled me, because I thought that the hearts of the children really should turn to the fathers, to the religion of the fathers. But that's not it! It says that the hearts of the fathers will be turned to the children in compassion. I think that may well have a connection, whether intentional or not, to this caring for the seventh generation.

FRITJOF: And I just wonder whether, in all this literature, beginning with Saint Francis of Assisi and various "ecological" saints, there wouldn't be something reminding us of this notion of sustainability. Sustainability, of course, was not a burning issue in past times, but today it is. So I think it would be worthwhile to look into this. This seems to be totally unexplored.

THOMAS: I think the Benedictine tradition has a rather good record in this area. Take, for example, the Hermitage of Camaldoli in the Italian Apennines. Very early in the history of that community, which dates back to the eleventh century, the constitution contained precise regulations regarding the cultivation of the forest. A solemn meeting with a vote was required for the cutting of any trees, and any trees that were cut had to be replanted. This regulation was written into the constitution of the monastic community not only because the forest was an economic resource but also because the monks had a sense of rootedness in the Earth, of their belonging to a particular place, which entailed the responsibility of making that place humanly livable for the future. The community was not limited to only one generation but was expected to continue throughout the centuries.

DAVID: René Dubos, the grandfather of ecological awareness, wrote a whole chapter in one of his books about Benedictine stewardship and about the role monastics played in this respect throughout the centuries.

FRITJOF: Another thing that comes to my mind is that previously in the conversation, when we talked about the nature of spirit, you said that all life is animated by the spirit of God. Many traditions say that the spirit of God sustains all life.

DAVID: You see that verbatim in the Book of Wisdom and in Psalm 104.

FRITJOF: So if the spirit of God, or the dance of Shiva, as the Hindus say, sustains all life and does it also in time and through time, then to act against this is really acting against the spirit of God. It's really a non-spiritual attitude. Then acting with sustainability in mind would be acting within the spirit of God.

DAVID: I think one could really say that sustainability, in the way you have described it, would be a decisive mark of a person who's really alive and alert to what spirituality demands in our time.

FRITJOF: The Hindu image of the dancing Shiva is very powerful and also very subtle. It includes both creation and destruction. So sustaining does not mean sustaining individual forms but the patterns of organization that form the fabric of life. Characteristically the third element in the dance of Shiva is sustaining.

DAVID: His third hand expresses this by the gesture of sustaining. This reminds me of the outstretched hands of Christ on the cross.

THOMAS: In what was perhaps the first compendium of the Catholic faith, a work called *Epideixis,* written toward the end of the second century by Saint Irenaeus, the cross is presented not only as the central event in human redemption but also as the center of the entire cosmos. The four arms of the cross unite height and depth, length and breadth, recapitulating both historical time and the cosmic cycles.

FRITJOF: I think this is still a rich field for theology to explore.

A spirituality of social responsibility

FRITJOF: In the very beginning of our conversation, you said, David, that spirituality for you is the way in which the religious experience flows into everyday life. I would like to discuss specific examples of how this would help us in solving the problems we face today.

DAVID: Fine. That can be relatively easy, because each of the shifts in theology is paralleled by a shift in spirituality that has considerable social relevance. I could pick out salvation, for instance. In the new paradigm salvation is no longer seen as a private affair. Formerly you could easily get the wrong impression that salvation was a private matter. Now, in this new holistic approach, the emphasis falls on its social implications.

FRITJOF: What exactly do you mean?

DAVID: When we speak of salvation, we are talking about the process of going from alienation to community. The key term in the message of Jesus is the "Kingdom of God." That doesn't mean heaven or any other particular place; translated into contemporary terminology, "Kingdom of God" means the experience of ultimate belonging plus the kind of society that results when we take our belonging seriously and act upon it.

If we take salvation in a holistic sense, as the new thinking in theology suggests, then we come back to the original understanding that the Kingdom is not only a change in my heart but a change in my heart that has all these social implications. I will then behave toward others as one behaves when one belongs. I will be a fully responsible member in the Earth Household.

FRITJOF: So the ethical implications of the sense of belonging would be an important part?

DAVID: Yes. That would be one aspect.

FRITJOF: This is very important to me because this is a difficulty for science. Although values are quite clearly part of the paradigm and therefore the driving force in scientific activity, scientific theory itself does not make statements about values. The scientific theory can tell you about the interconnectedness of all life, but then what follows from that in terms of behavior—as you say, when one belongs to a community, one behaves in a certain way—this is not something where science can really help. So the spiritual grounding would be important.

DAVID: That would be a good example for an area in which a scientist as scientist would have nothing to say; yet as a human being, the scientist has to say something, has to make a moral, a religious, commitment.

FRITJOF: Yes, and that is very important.

DAVID: So actually what you have pointed out is that when you come to talk about values, you have moved out of the limited realm of science proper into the larger realm of personal responsibility.

FRITJOF: Yes, but this is a tricky question. I'm not saying that values are not relevant to science.

DAVID: No. I understand you.

FRITJOF: But they're not part of the scientific theory. They are the background and the motivation for doing science, but they're really outside the scientific theory.

DAVID: What then do you have to say to the often-repeated statement that science is value-free?

FRITJOF: It's not value-free, because it's determined by values. What kind of research I do will depend on my value system, and it will be determined by society's value system, because the kind of research I do will depend on the kinds of grants I get.

DAVID: This seems to be one of those cases in which not to choose is to choose. If you say you are value-free, you are only following the dominant values.

FRITJOF: Absolutely. But let me come back to theology. What did you mean when you said that salvation is not an individual matter? Could you speak about this a little bit?

DAVID: I mean that salvation is not conceivable apart from its social implications. Not any longer. Up until very recently, for example, one would certainly have counseled a person to give alms, but one would hardly have encouraged anyone to look into the reason why the poor are poor and need alms. Now consciousness-raising of this kind has become quite explicit in sermons and in theological writings. In this new approach we ask about the underlying systemic problems and see an individual Christian's responsibility as directed toward systemic injustices.

FRITJOF: It's really interesting that in the new theology you would now look at the problems in a systemic way. What kinds of problems would they be?

DAVID: I've mentioned poverty. Respect for the environment would be another problem. War and peace would certainly belong here. All of this is largely linked with moral theology, but it must be seen in a much broader context. It is not just a question of whether I should pay taxes that are used for the arms race or whether I should be a conscientious objector. It's a new way of looking at the whole question of war. Is it necessary in our world to have wars? How can we solve our problems in other ways? Can we let our belonging be limited to the boundaries of our country?

FRITJOF: Traditionally the role of the pastor has been to deal with people's individual problems. Does this role still exist?

DAVID: Yes, it will always exist. To a certain extent that remains a function of the pastor, but the pastor's function as community coordinator is equally stressed today. Formerly the pastor in a Catholic parish was a sort of little monarch with absolute power. Now—in many places in fact and everywhere in theory—the pastor has a parish council that he merely coordinates. He takes responsibility for the final decision but ought to listen to the input of men and women in this parish council.

FRITJOF: In this pastoral activity, is there a sign of the same shift to look at problems systemically?

DAVID: Oh, yes, very much so. This is typical in what I would call the more alive churches. They will have committees for many different social concerns. You might find committees on prison reform, committees on racial justice, on housing, on the protection of Central American refugees.

FRITJOF: Now, this kind of systemic analysis is not really informed by spirituality. It seems that the churches have found a niche here because nobody else is doing it. If the politicians were doing it, I don't think the churches would have committees on racial injustice. If this were handled properly by politicians, then we wouldn't need that. A letter from the Catholic bishops on economics would not be necessary if economists and politicians got their act together. So in a sense the churches have jumped into a role here. This is not really informed by spirituality, but maybe just generally by social responsibility. In other words, if I drop in on a committee meeting on housing or social justice in a church, probably for a long time, I wouldn't be able to tell that this was a church.

DAVID: But is that necessary?

FRITJOF: No, it's not necessary. But for the sake of our discussion, these activities do not show me the social implications of the new view of spirituality.

THOMAS: I'm glad you raised this point. I have hesitated to come in on this topic up until now, first, because I understand David's underlying rationale, with which I substantially agree, and second, because I was expecting you, Fritjof, to question him as you just did. Here, in fact, is the crux of the issue: The new paradigm does not elaborate a spirituality that then has some social implications; it holds that spirituality is essentially and inevitably social. We are "spiritual," that is, united with God, in society with others or not at all. And these "others" are not only the members of our own religion but ultimately the whole human family. This is the oldest Christian paradigm of all, elaborated in the second century by the anonymous *Letter to Diognetus,* a great witness to early Christian universalism.

DAVID: Before the new way of thinking in theology, many people, perhaps the majority, were hung up on the need for private good deeds. Now we have a holistic, broader outlook in theology, a more communal understanding of salvation and of its social implications. Therefore countless people are engaged in these concerns. This is their spirituality.

FRITJOF: So this is part of the religious life?

DAVID: It's as much part of their religious life as, let's say, fasting or prayer. This is how they translate their religious awareness into every-day life.

FRITJOF: Now I understand it. This would correspond to the Zen say-ing that the practice of Zen is to carry water and chop wood.

DAVID: Exactly.

FRITJOF: Somebody unaware of Zen wouldn't see this as religious at all.

DAVID: It's interesting that you should have made this comment, as quite a number of Christians still in the old way of thinking are saying, "We want to have our good old-time religion back. Devotions, not acti-vism." One bishop is infamous for saying, "Pray the rosary for peace. Don't demonstrate." That would be exactly what you're talking about. There are some who don't understand. They say, "What are these people doing? They're Marxist activists. This has nothing to do with religion!" But in this holistic view, from a well-founded theological point of view, it has everything to do with religion. That's the way you live your religion.

Spirituality and creativity

DAVID: In the new thinking there is also a switch from salvation-centered theology to creation-centered theology.

FRITJOF: What does this mean, "creation-centered theology"?

DAVID: It's a theology that is not centered on the famous question of fundamentalists, "Are you saved?" Those who are on the forefront of the new thinking would answer, "Yes, thank God we have been saved. What next? How do you live out this saved life, this life of belonging?" That is why the emphasis falls on creation, both in the sense of the cosmos, the creation, and of your own creativity. In the former sense, "creation" is the theological term for "nature," for all created things.

FRITJOF: So you move to an emphasis on nature.

DAVID: And within that nature you emphasize your own creativity. After all, you are not a movable part of a cosmic machine but a cocreator. This is where responsible stewardship for our environment becomes, quite obviously, a religious responsibility.

FRITJOF: So, if you go to confession, instead of getting ten Hail Marys, you could be told, "Recycle your newspapers."

DAVID: It is not at all impossible that this could happen. Morally mature persons will, in the context of confession, accuse themselves not of the more superficial failings but will focus on actions that cause a rift in our belonging on a deeper level. In this context someone may well confess: "I have not really taken care of my environment. My block is a mess." Or something like that. Then the priest might say, "Recycle your newspapers." Today this is not a joke at all anymore. It fits into the framework of a new thinking in theology and of a new sense of responsibility in spirituality.

I know a good many nuns who, in addition to their traditional devotions, are now picking up aluminum cans with great devotion. They are selling them to help the poor. I know Benedictines in Minnesota who have raised thousands of dollars for the homeless in this way. They've really organized their project. It's a lot of work to store the cans and to crush them, and it's not very appetizing either. They do it out of religious conviction, yet it can be recognized by other people as something any decent human being should be willing to do in our time.

THOMAS: The Benedictine nuns' recycling project suggests that there is something in specifically monastic spirituality—in the Benedictine ethos but also perhaps in the Buddhist—that overcomes the apparent incompatibility of contemplation and social action. The services monks have rendered to society have nothing "activistic" about them; they are fruits of contemplation, *contemplata aliis tradere*, the overflow from their contemplative vision of the world.

FRITJOF: That makes a lot of sense to me. I see deep ecological awareness and spiritual awareness as flowing together, and recycling is a kind of discipline, a kind of asceticism in your sense of the term, that makes you sensitive toward living in cyclical processes within ecosystems; it therefore becomes the discipline for an ecological life. If an ecological life ultimately is a spiritual life, then it becomes a spiritual discipline.

DAVID: And by spiritual we mean, of course, fully alive, since spirit means life breath. The spirit is the life breath of God within us. If you're fully alive, alert, and responsive to the challenge of every moment, then you are living a spiritual life.

I had to give a short course on Christian spirituality once at Loreto Heights College in Denver, and on the first day I brought a stack of brown paper bags to class, one for each of the students.

"Let's clean up the campus," I said. "It is a mess. This is a spiritual activity, and you will learn more by doing it than I could teach you with words." They were so cooperative that toward the end of our course, the campus was spick and span. Finally they had to crawl under bushes and with sticks rake out paper cups and bottles; they just couldn't find any more rubbish to stuff in their bags. We made a real impact on the campus, and, in the discussion that followed, the students agreed that our environmental cleanup had taught them much about spirituality and about what it really means to be alive.

FRITJOF: To be mindful.

Global ecumenism and world peace

DAVID: I had a third point in mind. The first one was that through the switch toward holistic thinking in theology we come to a theology that is mindful of social issues. My second point was that through a switch to an emphasis on creation, you become aware of your ecological responsibility. My third point is that the new thinking in theology is strongly ecumenical. Formerly there may have been a tendency to stress what separates us from other religious traditions. The new thinking sees not so much difference as complementarity. When you think of your own way as the only possible way, you have to think of all the others as wrong. But if you think of your way as one particular approach to the divine reality, then you can think of the others as so many other valid perspectives. You will be grateful to have the variety and complementarity of different views enriching each other.

The new thinking stresses that common religious awareness, which unites us with others in their approach to divine reality. The more this awareness is being stressed, the more we realize our common ground, what unites us rather than what divides us.

THOMAS: My own experience of the interreligious dialogue has convinced me that this opening to people of other faiths and to the truth we seek and hold in common intensifies my personal commitment to truth as such. Ultimately what we all have in common is the human reality of living on this earth in a light that comes from beyond the earth and beyond our religions.

In dialogue I do not lose what is unique in my Christian faith, which is really Christ himself. Do I truly believe that the fullness of divinity dwelt in him bodily, as Saint Paul said? If I do, then I should turn to my Muslim brother or my Hindu sister or anyone and discover in their humanity the same divinity.

DAVID: Right! We prove that we see God in Jesus Christ by seeing God in every human being we meet.

FRITJOF: This of course could be extremely important politically, because we don't even have to go to other creeds. Just within the Christian community—in Northern Ireland or in Lebanon or to a lesser degree in Switzerland and Belgium—Catholics are fighting Protestants. Different cultural communities representing different branches of Christianity, are at war with each other.

DAVID: Of course, in all those cases, the deeply committed Christians are not the ones in the front lines; rather, they are the peacemakers. Think of the leverage religion could give to peace. All the religions in the world preach peace. If they would stand up united against this ridiculous waste of money on armaments, we'd have a better chance for peace. I think of the ecumenical thrust largely as a force of peacemaking. Religions have for too long a time been forces of discord in the world, in spite of the fact that they have all preached peace. If only religions could start making peace their common concern.

FRITJOF: Of course, this is happening now in many cases.

DAVID: In many cases, yes. That's a typical example of the new think-ing in theology bearing fruit. This could not possibly have happened without a shift of consciousness.

FRITJOF: An example that comes to my mind is the Protestant Church in Germany, both East and West, which has been on the forefront of the peace movement; also the majority of Catholic bishops in the United States; and from another culture, the Dalai Lama, who is an outstanding example of a Buddhist who is really on a mission of peace.

DAVID: One is also reminded of the historic meeting at Assisi: the pope sitting next to the Dalai Lama. The pope did not sit up on a throne, but they sat next to each other on the same level. Things like that really show that there's not just a new thinking in theology but that a real force for peace in the world flows from it, a powerful energy for social change. What we see at the top actually started at the grass roots. Just think of Benedictines for Peace in Erie, Pennsylvania, and similar cen-ters for justice and peace, the dawning of a new age.

The New Age movement

DAVID: Fritjof, this leads me to ask you, how do you define the New Age movement?

FRITJOF: In Europe nowadays I am always asked this question. I define it as a particular manifestation of the social paradigm shift, a manifesta-tion that flourished in California in the 1970s and no longer exists in its original form. It was a particular constellation of concerns, interests, and topics—the human potential movement, the whole field of humanistic psychology, the interest in spirituality, in the occult, in paranormal phenomena, and the holistic health movement. I would say that those together were called the New Age movement, and what characterized them in the negative sense was the practically total absence of social and political consciousness. While there was, of course, a strong environmental movement in California in the 1970s, there was neither ecological consciousness nor social consciousness in the sense of citizens' movements à la Ralph Nader. Nor was there femi-nist consciousness. All of this was absent from the New Age movement.

In the 1980s this changed quite a bit. These various holistic therapists and humanistic psychologists embraced the concerns of the peace movement, of the women's movement, of various other social movements, to the extent that they don't want to be called New Agers any longer. So I tell people in Europe that when we use the term *New Age* now, we mostly use it to talk about people who are still New Agers, who are stuck in the consciousness of the 1970s.

THOMAS: Maybe we should just let the term *New Age* drop. Certainly it rings all the wrong bells in the minds of mainstream Christians.

DAVID: It's a pity, though, to leave this meaningful term to a historic period. The good news always calls for a New Age.

THOMAS: Of course the expression New Age and its underlying symbolism—although not its theoretical content—echo similar expressions in the Bible. The idea of a New Age is also part of the American myth. Take that Latin phrase *Novus ordo saeclorum* on all our dollar bills—what does it mean but "New Age"?

FRITJOF: In Europe you can talk about a New Age movement, I think, but here you can't talk about it in terms of a dynamic movement, because it's not. And of course the question then is, What do you call it? I would love to be able to call it the Green movement, because that's what the Green movement should be, but it isn't.

DAVID: I would say that the Association for Humanistic Psychology (AHP), for example, has a New Age consciousness, a full New Age consciousness. And in that sense you can reintroduce this term.

FRITJOF: Of course, the values of the New Age movement are still valid and as important now as they were then.

DAVID: But to bring about an age that is really new, these values have to be augmented by others that were not appreciated at first.

FRITJOF: Right. They are enlarged by enlarging the transpersonal consciousness into the social.

Liberation theologies

FRITJOF: Both of you have mentioned liberation theology several times in our conversation in connection with grass-roots movements. Could you say a little more about this movement? What intrigues me also in this connection is the Eastern idea of liberation as spiritual liberation, as enlightenment; for example, the Hindu concept of *moksha*. I wonder whether there's any connection.

DAVID: There surely is. But before we go on, let's be careful to speak of liberation theologies in the plural rather than liberation theology. There's a whole variety of liberation theologies.

THOMAS: We should also remember that the various liberation theologies are not particularly original with regard to their content. Often, on the great themes of Christian faith, the Trinity, the incarnation, and so forth, they're very traditional, very middle-of-the-road, you might say. But it's the method that's all-important.

The method begins with the experience of people who are in captivity; it makes its starting point a reflection on the condition of the poor, the powerless, marginal people, those trapped in a system of institutionalized violence. This initial reflection gives the theologian a key to understanding what the Bible and Christian tradition say about salvation. Liberation theology sees revelation and salvation as one and the same process: God is revealed in the fact that people who were once enslaved and oppressed have been set free and have entered into justice.

It's been said that there's a risk of reductionism in liberation theology—aside from any Marxist influences, which are minor in my estimation—and that it tends to make liberation solely a social or economic thing. This risk may be present in some individuals, but the really serious liberation theologians, Gustavo Gutiérrez or Leonardo Boff, for example, are convinced of the value of prayer and the value of the inner experience. The simple people in the grass-roots communities, especially in Brazil, spontaneously develop a contemplative spirit. A vision of reality in the light of the liberating God leads them to perceive the roots of their oppression and to overcome it. Contemplative wisdom leads to social action.

So liberation theology is a method of listening to the way the oppressed listen to the word of God. It's not a new method; you can find something very similar in Pope Gregory the Great and other early Christian writers.

DAVID: Let me suggest this thought: The primary liberation, the primary reason these theologies deserve to be called liberation theologies, is that the simple people in the grass-roots communities are freed to do theology, which formerly was just handed on to them by professional theologians.

THOMAS: Of course, we are not talking about the professional theology of the schools. In other words, this understanding of faith, this reflection on God's self-manifestation in history, is done by the people and with the people. The liberation theologians listen to the people and to their experiences and then use the people's expressions in formulating the understanding of faith.

DAVID: It certainly comes from the people rather than out of the books.

THOMAS: It's based on the supposition that the theme of liberation is a great dominant thread running through the whole of revelation.

DAVID: And the first event that set the whole thing in motion was the exodus and the liberation of the people from Egypt.

THOMAS: Exactly.

DAVID: What we find in our Bibles preceding the Book of Exodus is actually a reflection on the exodus experience, even the story of creation is told in the light of Israel's great liberation.

THOMAS: Yes. It's important to remember that the Book of Genesis was written *after* the experience of the exodus from Egypt; some of it much later, toward the end of the Babylonian exile, a thousand years after the event.

FRITJOF: So the "early" books of the Bible are actually relatively late?

THOMAS: Yes. They are liberation accounts told with an eye on the liberation from Egypt. In other words, once we have experienced in the exodus that God saves us from slavery, we look back on our history and its origins and see the same power of God operating throughout.

FRITJOF: Can you say, then, that liberation is a key element in the Old Testament?

DAVID: Absolutely *the* key!

THOMAS: Even in the New Testament the theme of exodus is important.

DAVID: It is also important to recognize that wherever the word *judgment* occurs, where God is presented as judge, that, too, is a reference to liberation. The judgment of God does not mean that God sits, as we sometimes envisage, and judges as in a courtroom. Judgment in the Hebrew Bible means that God helps the poor gain their rights, liberates them from oppression. Therefore the notion of God as judge should be a joyful one. Wherever the people are oppressed, God's judgment is indeed longed for as liberation. Only in those churches where the oppressors get together is God's judgment something to be feared. You can tell from the overtones of the word *judgment* in what kind of church you are, the poor or the rich church.

FRITJOF: So this theme of liberation in the Old Testament was then taken up by various oppressed peoples.

DAVID: It was first taken up by Jesus.

FRITJOF: Right, let's talk about that first. What is liberation in the New Testament?

DAVID: What we call redemption is in plain English liberation. We have developed a whole set of words for Sunday use that are different from the words for everyday use; we have domesticated terms that in their original meaning are too uncomfortable for us. What would be another example?

THOMAS: Salvation.

DAVID: Yes, salvation really means healing, healing on every level, especially healing of alienation. Righteousness is another one of those Sunday words; it tries to soften the impact of the word justice.

FRITJOF: What is the political background and how does it relate to the spiritual message of Jesus?

DAVID: Apparently the political situation at the time of Jesus was quite similar to the situation in places like Central America right now, where liberation theologies are springing up.

FRITJOF: I see. Thus the embarrassment.

DAVID: Thus the embarrassment. Jesus is certainly a political figure and has a political message, but not in terms of party politics. This is, of course, difficult to reconstruct, but it's fairly safe to say that he tries to stay out of party politics. Yet it is clear to him and to everyone else concerned that his message is quite explosive politically.

FRITJOF: What was this revolutionary message?

DAVID: I would say it is clear from the Gospels that Jesus causes an authority crisis.

FRITJOF: On what authority does Jesus base his stance?

DAVID: The answer is not, as is sometimes assumed, that Jesus stands on his own charismatic authority; nor does he base his claims directly on God's authority as if God were standing behind him. Unlike the prophets, Jesus never says, "Thus says the Lord." So to what authority does he appeal? Yes, he appeals to the divine authority, but in the hearts of his hearers. That is something completely new. He bases his whole teaching on the fact that every single one of his hearers—even the harlots, the tax collectors, the outcasts, the shepherds who had no rights, the women who had no voice—has God's own voice speaking in his or her heart. He never goes around saying, "I will tell you what to do. Listen, and I will give you advice." He goes around telling parables.

That is his typical teaching method. The parables Jesus uses work like jokes. Often he starts with a question, like, "Who of you fishermen doesn't know; who of you women baking bread doesn't know; who of you who goes out sowing seed doesn't know?" "You know, don't you?" That's the first step. We, the hearers, reply, "Of course we all know. Common sense tells us so." But now the joke is on us, for Jesus asks, "Ah, if common sense tells you what to do, then why don't you act accordingly?" Jesus' parables hinge on common sense, on that spirit we have received so that we may know God from within. The parables presuppose that we can know God's mind through such simple activities as fishing, bread baking, or sowing seed—know God's mind and live accordingly.

But why would anyone *not* live by that common sense which we share with all humans, animals, plants, with the whole universe and with its divine ground? Why don't we live by that spirit which we have in common and which alone makes sense? Because we are intimidated by public pressure, public opinion. Jesus drives a wedge between common sense and public pressure. By his parables, he says to people, "Don't give in to that pressure! You know better." He builds them up, he makes them stand on their own two feet. Sometimes, literally. When people get enthusiastic, they trust so much in that power that they can get up and walk even though they were lame before. Stories like that in the Gospels still have power today to change people's lives.

Yet anybody who empowers others in that way immediately gets in trouble with those authorities who put people down, with religious as well as political authoritarians. We read quite explicitly in the earliest Gospel accounts that the common folk were amazed. They said, "This man speaks with authority, not like our authorities!" Of course, this sort of thing doesn't sit well with oppressive authorities. What is more liberating than common sense?

FRITJOF: Let me ask you something. I have read several times in comparisons between Christianity and Buddhism that liberation is a key term in both religions, but that the way they go about it is very different. The symbol of liberation in Christianity is Jesus on the cross, who saves us through his death, while the symbol of Buddhism is the Buddha in meditation, who shows us that we can do it ourselves. The Buddha never said he will save us. He says, "If you want to be liberated, I'll show you how to do it. You can do it yourself." That kind of empowerment.

According to what you are saying, this also somehow was the message of Jesus. It was not, "I'll die on the cross, and you'll be saved."

DAVID: I agree, but there is in every religious tradition the tendency to move from the teacher who empowers you, saying, "You can do it!" toward putting this teacher higher and higher up on a pedestal until you only rely on the teacher. You have this tendency in Buddhism, too. In the Pure Land school, all you need to do is call upon Buddha and Buddha will save you. I think that originally both Jesus and Buddha "saved" people by empowering them. But, well, this is a delicate topic.

THOMAS: It's a delicate topic because their respective teachings are expressed in very different literary genres, very different languages. The conceptual universes of Buddhism and Christianity are so different one from the other that it's almost impossible to bring the two religions down to a common denominator on the question of the Teacher's authority. I think, though, that you would have to admit that in the New Testament an important element in the teaching of Jesus is simply "To you, the poor, is given the Kingdom." This is central to the message of Jesus.

DAVID: Yes. You are right. Maybe I tend to polarize too much the teaching *of* Jesus over against the teaching *about* Jesus. I see your point. However, even the Gospel of John, which contains the most highly developed teaching *about* Jesus, makes it clear that every follower of Jesus should come to be able to say, "I and the Father are one." For each one of his followers Jesus prays, according to John, that he or she may be able to say *with* Jesus, "I and the Father are one." This may sound outrageous to some Christian ears, but it is John's way of speaking of the Kingdom of God.

FRITJOF: The conventional view is that the Church says to the poor, "Yes, the Kingdom of God is given to you. But it's after you die. In the meantime, go to Church and be good. But don't meddle with politics." That's not a message of empowerment.

DAVID: If by Church, you mean the religious establishment, then you have given a pretty accurate description. Religious institutions are always in danger of aligning themselves with the ruling classes. The Church as institution was helping the poor as well as it could. But it tended to forget that the poor *are* the Church. God's Kingdom belongs to the poor. Dom Helder Camara says, "If you help the poor, they call you a saint. But if you ask why the poor are poor, they call you a communist." That is why some of the most truly Christlike figures in Central America today are branded as communists, even bishops.

FRITJOF: So what are the modern liberation theologies? Did the term arise just a few years ago in Central America?

THOMAS: Yes, it comes from the title of a book by Gustavo Gutiérrez: *A Theology of Liberation.* Gutiérrez's expression gave a name to a movement that was already beginning to emerge in various places, especially in Brazil. There the alliance of the Church with the landowners and the military had demonstrated its inevitable failure. So some theologians began to ask, "What are we going to do? Where is the population going to go? Is it going to become completely secularized? Is it going to adopt Marxist ideology?" The conclusion was "Let us listen to the people. Let *them* tell us what *their* reading of the gospel is and how the gospel can come alive for them."

FRITJOF: So it's a grass-roots theology.

THOMAS: It's the attitude of listening to the people as they listen to the word of God.

DAVID: There are also Ernesto Cardenal's books, in which he simply recounts, volume after volume, what simple Nicaraguan campesinos say in response to certain Gospel passages and how they depict the stories. That is truly inspiring; it has moved many people.

FRITJOF: What *do* they say? What are some of the key points of those liberation theologies? You said at the beginning, it's not so much what they say. Still, how do they talk about liberation?

DAVID: For instance, they say that salvation or liberation is for them not something that affects only the soul while everything else stays the way it was. They apply Jesus' good news to their concrete situation, to such things as co-ops and credit unions, labor unions, and things like that.

THOMAS: The most obvious insight in the gospel is that Jesus is the savior of the whole person, not only of the soul, and always of the individual within the community. Salvation is holistic or it is not salvation. It's not salvation if it separates people from people.

FRITJOF: In my studies of Buddhism, I often had the following thought. The Buddha says, "Life is suffering, and here is the way out, the Eightfold Path." This refers to psychological suffering, to the existential human condition. It does not deal with the suffering that is caused by injustice. I have often thought that you have to distinguish between the two. For the suffering caused by injustice, the remedy is political action; for the psychological suffering, the remedy is the Eightfold Path. It seems that in this liberation theology, the two are coming together. Liberation is liberation from both.

DAVID: Yes, and therefore, for instance, in Vietnam, at the time of the war, the Christians and the Buddhists who understood this felt very close to one another. It was not called liberation theology at that time, but it was similar. I remember Thich Nhat Hanh telling me about it. He's a great Vietnamese Buddhist monk, a writer, poet, and peace activist. He told me that during those years in Vietnam, he and his coworkers often felt much closer to Christian priests and lay people who were working with them as peace activists than to other Buddhists in their establishment.

FRITJOF: So there *is* a connection between the two kinds of liberation, the spiritual and the political?

DAVID: Definitely. There is a connection between spirituality and *every* dimension of life. Spirituality is not a special department; it is a higher intensity of aliveness. One's measure of freedom is a measure of one's aliveness. Since life is of one piece, one's inner aliveness must express itself in outer aliveness; one's inner freedom, in political freedom. To the extent that you are liberated in your heart, you are sensitized to the need for communal liberation and feel responsible for it.

THOMAS: Let's remember that liberation theology is at present no longer limited to the Latin American situation; it's open now to a wide variety of issues: interreligious, sexual, ecological. What remains constant is a theological method that is typically new paradigm: the grass-roots element, the emphasis on the total human person, on overcoming the philosophical ambiguities of the soul/body language, and on the historical process. In other words, liberation theology sees revelation as the process of God's saving presence in the concrete, human, historical reality; it's a theology about creating actual human communities of freedom and equality, animated by a strong and profound hope that points to justice both in this world and in the Kingdom of God's eternity.

DAVID: Liberation theology also overcomes the dichotomy of thought and action. Gandhi accomplished this, too.

Authority and power

FRITJOF: Among all the people in the world who have done peace and social-change work based on a spiritual grounding, Gandhi is certainly a shining example. Gandhi's work shows us in a very dramatic way somebody who knew how to deal with power without being corrupted by power.

In my experience, one of the great problems faced by grass-roots movements today, and by social activists who want to change things in the world, is the dilemma of political power. It arises in various ways. Should we make deals with people or with organizations in political power, with political parties, for example? Should we thereby assume power? And how can we do this without being corrupted? We know that power corrupts.

Another aspect is that the grass-roots organizations themselves, to the extent that they become political, have to deal with power among themselves. You could almost say that by definition the political arena is the arena of power. A central aspect of politics is the distribution of power.

Since we know that power corrupts and that power has all kinds of negative side effects, and since we know that Gandhi was one who was able to deal with power in an exemplary way and was a deeply spiritual person, what does that tell us about the relationship between spirituality and power? This whole question of spirituality and power is, I think, an extremely important one.

DAVID: I would like to address myself to that, but I usually speak of it in the terms of authority. If we look up the definition of authority, we find "power to command." Then you ask, "Where did this power to command come from? Who gave it to the authorities?" This leads you to the basic meaning of authority; namely authority as "a firm basis for knowing and acting." That's very different from "power to command." But it's the original notion of authority. When you are researching, you want to have not just hearsay but a firm basis for knowing; so you go to an authoritative book. When you are seriously ill, you go to a doctor who is an authority in the particular field of medicine connected with your troubles. We do use the word *authority* also in the sense of a firm basis for knowing and acting, but we have almost forgotten that this is its original meaning.

FRITJOF: So how does one get from authority meaning "a firm basis of knowing and acting" to authority meaning "power to command"?

DAVID: That step is relatively easy to understand, particularly on a small scale in society. Think, for instance, of a village or a tribe in earlier times. A person who proved to be a reliable basis for knowing and acting would be put in a position of authority. This still happens in a family. The authority figure may be some wise aunt to whom everyone goes when they have questions. She is put in a position of authority. In Native American society, they had their war chiefs. When there was an emergency, they looked around for a person who had often been a reliable source of knowing and acting, and they made that person a chief. But when the war was over, when the emergency was past, that person went back into the ranks.

THOMAS: That is a very sensible way of dealing with authority, which you find also in the early history of the people of Israel after the exodus from Egypt. The Book of Judges tells of the temporary charismatic leaders who called the twelve tribes together at times of crisis and led them in battle. One of these "judges" was in fact a woman, Deborah.

DAVID: More often, however, when persons get power to command, they establish themselves in power and maintain that position long after they have ceased to be a firm basis for knowing and acting. That is the turning point from genuine authority to authoritarian authority. We speak of someone being invested with authority. Investing means putting on vestments. The one so invested may or may not be a reliable source for acting or knowing, but in either case the vestment gives power to command.

Two things have to come together to keep authority healthy: strength and accountability. In other words, those who wield power must be responsible for their use of power. Authoritarianism comes about when people in power are no longer accountable. Accountability obliges you to respond to those who question authority. They may be so oppressed and exploited that they can't say anything; yet their very existence questions authority. What are we doing about it with our own power? It's important for us to remember that each one of us wields authority. In a family, in the place where we work, among our peers— everyone has a certain amount of authority.

FRITJOF: So we are really not talking about something out there— "they," those villains, those authoritarians. We are talking about ourselves.

DAVID: Yes. And here it begins to get interesting for me. The question What is the responsibility of those who wield authority? is addressed to all of us, though in different ways and degrees. My answer is, those in authority should use their power to empower those under their authority, to make them stand on their own two feet. To empower someone means giving them authority; and to give someone authority means giving them responsibility. That is why the coward in each of us doesn't want authority; we simply don't want the responsibility that goes with it. By shirking our own responsibility we play into the hands of authoritarians.

FRITJOF: This process of having authority and having others under authority, and having to empower them as the only viable solution, is always with us and was always with us in parenting. Whether they like it or not in whatever situation, the parents offer the small child a reliable source for acting and knowing. This little scenario is played out whenever anything is going on; gradually they have to make this child stand on her own two feet. Hand on authority to her, or rather empower her to use the authority that is within her. The process of parenting all over the world is the process in which we learn these things. But we also learn that the child very soon—and that means each one of us—wants the power but not the responsibility! That is what gives us all these problems about authority.

DAVID: What can we do about this? What can we do about our willingness to sell out to those in power because it is easier than taking responsibility upon ourselves. This is the real problem.

THOMAS: Just look at how few people take responsibility and go to the polls in this country. Such a simple thing to do.

DAVID: And the majority of those who do not go to vote complain about the authorities. They are so dissatisfied with the candidates that they don't even bother to vote. It doesn't matter who wins; one will be as good as the other.

THOMAS: They'd rather say that one would be as bad as the other so there's no point in going to vote. But in a democracy, the real reason for voting is not so much to choose this or that candidate as it is to express your convictions and join your vote to that of others who share them.

DAVID: Yes, that's how you exercise your authority responsibly in a democracy.

With regard to authority, our society has a blind spot. Most people will simply not believe that the human being gladly bows to authority. Our society believes that everybody is really at heart a rebel, unless you keep them under control. Parents already treat the child as a potential rebel. But the child is not a rebel; a bit unruly, that's all; the child wants power. But the real problem is not that the child wants power; the real problem is that the child doesn't want to bear responsibility. I just remind you of the experiments that Stanley Milgram made at Yale. He showed that large numbers of ordinary people were ready to commit violence when asked to do so by an authority figure. I think the reason for that shocking result is that people would rather be powerless than rise to their responsibility.

FRITJOF: So what can we do about that?

DAVID: Here it becomes helpful to ask, How did Jesus teach before the Church began to teach *about* Jesus? Historians generally agree that he taught with authority and that he empowered his hearers. He empowered the little people. They said—and this is mentioned several times in the Gospels—"This man speaks with authority." Then they added, "But not like our authorities." This compassion got him in trouble. When somebody speaks to your heart and says things you always knew, but didn't quite dare to put into words, you say, "Oh, this person really speaks with authority." And that's what they said about Jesus. He authorized them to trust their inmost religious awareness. He reminded them of the God they knew in their heart of hearts: God as a loving father, as a mother hen gathering her chicks under her wings. He showed them what they had always known deep inside: that God loves each one of us as if we were the only one, and all of us as one big family. Jesus made outcasts his friends and gave them a sense of belonging. He brought about healing, not by saying, "Zap, you're healed," but by giving them trust in the divine healing power within them: "Your faith—your trust—has made you well!" He didn't say, "Zap! Your sins are forgiven," but he reminded them of what their hearts knew: that God's love had forgiven their sins before they ever sinned. But someone who builds up the self-respect of the common folk is a thorn in the side of those who keep themselves in power by putting others down.

For the individual believer, one of the most important switches in the new thinking of theology is that it gives full weight to personal experience of the divine. Every teaching needs to be linked to one's own religious awareness. Formerly it was from outside and from above that religious verities were handed to you.

The question an adult is asked before baptism is, "What do you ask from the Church?" That is the crucial question, and the answer is "Faith." In the old-paradigm thinking that means "Hand me all the verities of faith. Give me the package." In the new understanding it means "Support me in my trusting exploration into God." These are two completely different attitudes. The moment you make this switch, you have acknowledged that the function of religious authority is the empowerment of the divine authority in all those who are under authority.

FRITJOF: This shows us that power and authority are very closely linked. Let us think of a doctor, for example. In the old paradigm the doctor is the authority on the patient's health. The doctor has the power to decide whether you are healthy or not and has the power to decide what to do with you if you are not healthy. So he will say, "You need an operation." Okay, so you go and have the operation. Or, "You need to take these medicines," so you go take the medicines.

DAVID: This is still prevalent.

FRITJOF: In the new paradigm the doctor acts much more as a counselor and as an assistant to the process of healing, which is really organized by the patient. The individual responsibility for health is much greater. So power and responsibility really go together, don't they?

Power and responsibility

FRITJOF: To me the questioning of authority was the common thread that wove through most of the 1960s movements. You had students questioning the authority of their teachers and of the university administration. In the Civil Rights movement, you had blacks questioning the authority of whites. In the women's movement, women questioning the authority of men. In the Prague spring, the Czechs questioning the authority of the Soviets. You had patients questioning the authority of their therapists. Does something like this exist in theology?

DAVID: Very much so. Theology has always asked questions. But they were asked within a certain framework and that framework was unquestionable. Now that framework is being questioned. For instance, formerly we discussed revelation by asking what was meant by a particular doctrine, but now you ask whether revelation is a set of doctrines or something else. You're suddenly going outside the frame that used to be taken for granted.

FRITJOF: In other words, you're questioning the paradigm. That comes with the whole notion of a paradigm, that you can question the context. The context is not something absolute; it is culturally and historically conditioned. And when you question the paradigm, you are also questioning authority, don't you think so?

DAVID: Yes, at least when the authorities insist on a given paradigm.

FRITJOF: When it is embodied in the social institutions. By questioning the paradigm, you question the social institutions.

DAVID: You question everything, radically yet reverently or respectfully. The paradigm in this context is the ultimate framework for your looking at things. But those words "radically yet reverently or respectfully" are critically important. And it is not easy to sustain the tension between the two attitudes when we question authority. It is important to respect earlier insights, earlier formulations of truth, earlier paradigms, even after we have moved on. They often carry some hard-won evidence and can correct blind spots, lacunae, misconceptions, and limitations of our present outlook. The Hebrew prophets used the ancient Torah to challenge the establishment of their time. The early Christians used the sayings of the prophets alongside those of Jesus to challenge the authorities of their time. We, in turn, use their words to challenge today's Church.

THOMAS: Could we say, then, that we must question not only those in positions of responsibility but also ourselves, to call forth our own response and sense of responsibility?

DAVID: Yes, indeed. The term *responsibility* implies that those whom we entrust with power must respond when they are questioned about the use of that power. It implies also that we must make use of our right to question them.

FRITJOF: Now, in old-paradigm politics, you say the government is responsible for this and that and therefore has the power to decide what to do with the tax money. The government is responsible for our security, for example, and it has the power to decide what kind of weapons we shall have. Whether security could mean something totally different is not asked. From the theological and religious point of view, how would you talk about responsibility?

DAVID: This is something that has been worked out very carefully in the Church's teaching. The technical term for the underlying principle is *subsidiarity*. In everyday language that means grass-roots decision making. The essence of the principle of subsidiarity is that any decision that can be made on a lower level must be made on that level, and it must be referred to the next higher level of authority only if the lower level can not deal with it adequately.

THOMAS: You could say that this principle, although rooted in the New Testament, has been made explicit only in relatively recent times. It all started with the so-called social encyclicals, beginning with Leo XIII's *Rerum Novarum* in the late nineteenth century, in which the principle of subsidiarity was applied to secular society but not to the Church's own structures, conceived as a pyramid in which everything came from the top down. The exception was and remains the Benedictine Order.

DAVID: We Benedictines are proud of this. One of the difficulties in applying the principle of subsidiarity however, is that the lower authorities are often so fearful that they gladly pass the power they should use on to the higher level of authority. We can't presume that people are always trying to get more power on the local level. Often they're all too happy to give it up. The bishops, for instance, frequently check back with Rome on cases that Rome wanted them to decide on their own.

THOMAS: This is especially true of the so-called Third Church in Asia and Africa. Although the Second Vatican Council fully authorized the "enculturation" of preaching and worship, their adaptation to local styles and customs, most Asian and African bishops hesitate to take any concrete steps in this direction without explicit Vatican approval.

FRITJOF: Coming back now to the relationship between power and spirituality, how do you see Gandhi's spirituality? Do you agree that he's an excellent example of how to handle power without being corrupted? And if so, what can we learn from that?

DAVID: Gandhi is recognized by many Christians as a Christlike figure. He did what Jesus most typically did, namely, empower others. That is what got Jesus into trouble, and that is also what got Gandhi into trouble.

FRITJOF: Yes, both of them were killed.

DAVID: In both cases the people didn't really want the power that was offered to them; not to that extent. Some did, but many others said, "We were much better off when we were told what to do. Under the British everything went smoothly."

FRITJOF: But those were not the people who killed Gandhi.

DAVID: That is true. If Jesus would have had a strong enough following of people who were willing to be empowered, they may have been able to protect him. I don't know in Gandhi's case. What I so admire in him is that, like Jesus, he used his power to empower others. According to the Gospels, that is the Christian use of power. The washing of his disciples' feet before the Last Supper is a typical example. Jesus said, "Worldly potentates rule it over their subjects. With you, it should be the other way around. The most powerful should be the servant of all."

FRITJOF: Here again, power goes together with responsibility.

DAVID: Right. Where power is separated from responsibility, it is corrupted. That would almost be the way of describing what corrupt power is.

FRITJOF: Now, we all know that responsibility is difficult. The more responsibility you have, the harder it is. Therefore, a responsible person who accumulates power will try to empower others so as to distribute the responsibility, decentralize responsibility, right? Because one can't handle too much of it. So if you accumulate power, there are only two ways of exercising it. One way is by clinging to power. This is not being responsible, it is corrupt power, which is of course what most power is. You go into power for power's sake. The other one is when you say, "I have too much power, too much responsibility, and I need to distribute it." And so you use your power to empower others. And that, you say, would be the Christian way of using power to empower others.

DAVID: Yes. But I wouldn't call it exclusively Christian; it's the common-sense way. If you asked me what the genuinely Christian influence has been over two thousand years, this new thing through which Christianity has transformed the West, it is precisely a new vision of power. This has caused turmoil from the beginning; it created martyrs. Often it has not been upheld by the authorities and power structures of the Church itself. But the ideal has been handed on. It is often espoused by people who do not stand within the Church, but it is recognizable as something that goes back in the history of the human mind to Jesus. In this respect he made an impact that is still reverberating in our time.

FRITJOF: In my lectures and seminars, I have often used the word *power* in two senses: power as dominating others and power as influencing others. Influence is more in the sense of empowering, and domination is more in the sense of corrupt power. The way this links to authority is that the true authority, in the original sense of the term, would be somebody who embodies trust and therefore is given responsibility, right?

DAVID: And should be given power as long as that person deserves that trust. But most authorities with power tend to hang on to it long after they deserve the trust.

FRITJOF: And the role of the authority is really to spread the knowledge so that people can help themselves and don't need others to rely on.

DAVID: Yes, that's what I mean when I say that authority is given for the empowerment of those under authority. Ultimately even when we recognize a religious authority out there, we do this on the strength of the divine authority, the ultimate authority, which we experience in our hearts.

FRITJOF: The other way this qualifies as new-paradigm thinking is that it's a dynamic notion. In the old paradigm, power is static. You have a rigid hierarchy, domination by the top level of all the other levels underneath. But if you see power as a constant flow outward to empower others and to strengthen their authority, that's a dynamic process.

DAVID: That's a very good point. Also, of course, the networking of authorities among different individuals, among different groups, not only vertically but also horizontally. Just think of computer networking as an expansion of power, access, input, and so forth in business, academia, personal life.

FRITJOF: This is why I say that the ideal structure for power as influence is the network. You get feedback not in the hierarchy but in the network.

THOMAS: The Catholic tradition has a theological basis for this kind of structure: the principle of collegiality, in which pope and bishops, clergy and laity act organically, as a living body, with distinct but interdependent functions attributed to the various members. Even the pope's barring priests from joining political parties and running for office can be understood as an affirmation of collegiality; direct responsibility for the secular realm belongs to lay people. They are the ones who should translate Christian ideals into political action. The Solidarity movement in Poland is an obvious example, although personally I feel greater admiration for someone like Václav Havel in Czechoslovakia.

World federalism

DAVID: With your statement, Thomas, we have come back to the principle of subsidiarity. In a healthy society, decisions should be made on the lowest level possible. Higher authority should step in only when necessary, but then it should step in. At present the highest political authority is invested in national governments. We do not yet have any authority with the power and the responsibility to deal with global issues. We do not yet have global authority. The closest we come to it is the United Nations, but it does not have the necessary power. Still, even with the limited power that the U.N. has, this organization has achieved a great deal already.

FRITJOF: I think the United Nations is a good example. It does not have power in the sense of domination and coercion of others, but it has a lot of power and a lot of authority in the sense of empowerment. The way it exerts this authority is by maintaining service agencies, such as UNICEF and peacekeeping forces, and a forum in which nations can meet. Today the greatest significance of the United Nations is as a forum for nongovernmental organizations.

DAVID: The United Nations does many extremely helpful things, but it is not able to do what we need in our world today because it operates on the principle of a league. In a league the members have not committed themselves. They can step out and just go their own way. In a federation the member states have submitted to a higher authority in those areas in which that authority really is necessary, and since it is necessary, they can no longer withdraw.

FRITJOF: Let me tell you the way I see this. I have often heard this notion of a world federation or a world government.

DAVID: Be careful not to call it government, because that raises specters of authoritarianism.

FRITJOF: But I want to talk about world government exactly to raise that specter. It's important to be clear on this. What you don't want is a centralized government. We don't even want this within the nations, because centralization is a major stumbling block today. So we want the nation states to undergo two kinds of developments. One is to decentralize power and economic activity, decentralize the decision-making process as much as possible within the state. The other one is to engage in far more substantive cooperation internationally with other states. If you follow those two developments, you'll get an overall federation where the decentralized decisions are coordinated. The role of this federation would be one of coordination, not of imposing its will.

THOMAS: I think that what needs to be constituted is an effective forum, charged with maintaining many levels of linkage, networking, and communication among government and nongovernment bodies, as well as among the regions within larger nation-states.

FRITJOF: In this connection it's fascinating for me to observe the developments in Western and Eastern Europe, which seem to go in opposite directions. In the West the European nations are saying, "We are too independent. We need to be more interdependent," and in the East they are saying, "We are too dependent on Moscow. We need to be more independent." I can very well imagine a scenario where the Eastern bloc countries will become more and more independent, and the Western bloc countries will become more and more interdependent. Once they have reached the same level of interdependence, they may just drop the Eastern and Western distinctions and unify, and they will be one community of interdependent countries.

DAVID: From a certain point on, the increase in interdependence is the basis for a greater and greater independence. There's a possibility of greater variety. The possibility for pluralism rises with unification.

THOMAS: Exactly. One might note that certain internal problems within European nation-states—I'm thinking especially of the conflict between the French government and the movement for autonomy on the Mediterranean island of Corsica—can be resolved only by this higher level of integration.

FRITJOF: Or the problems of Yugoslavia, the Basque desire for independence from Spain and France, the Baltic problems for the Soviets, and so on.

DAVID: I would very much like to find ways in which one could alert those many people of goodwill to the need to work in this direction, to world authority, world federalism rightly understood.

FRITJOF: I think there is a growing awareness, although people usually don't call it world federalism. They are talking about solving global problems with the help of global agencies.

DAVID: This is probably even better. But we need global agencies with authority.

FRITJOF: And I would say they don't need to be powerful in the first sense of power, having authority in the old-paradigm sense. For instance, Amnesty International is a very powerful organization, and it doesn't dominate anybody; it just influences people.

THOMAS: I would like to add that the term *interdependence* was adopted quite early on by John Paul II. And, I should add, the Holy See has been on the public record for decades as supporting a common world authority that would guarantee that war would no longer be waged among nations. This is one point where the Vatican's position was ahead of other religious groups and even of many conservative Catholics, especially in America.

DAVID: And here we are, at a point where John Paul II and Gorbachev share the same goals.

THOMAS: The coincidence of language is an overwhelming indication that each one reads the other.

Mikhail Gorbachev's new thinking

FRITJOF: Let me add something about Gorbachev, since you mentioned his name. When Gorbachev started the movement of perestroika, the Soviets became keenly aware that the goal of restructuring the Soviet economy would not be to move from a regulated economy to a free economy, because there's no such thing as a free economy. There are no free markets. So for the Soviet Union today, the question is not to move from a regulated economy to a free-market economy but from one type of regulation to another type of regulation. All economies are regulated, and they are regulated largely by cultural constraints. The Japanese form of capitalism is very different from the Swedish form, very different from the American form, very different from the German form, and so on. So the Soviets are now engaged in a broad exploration of what kind of regulation they should use.

Now comes the interesting point. Gorbachev realized around 1988 that when they talked about moving from one kind of regulation to another kind of regulation, they wanted a regulation by which people would agree to do certain things and not do other things. To enforce that kind of regulation, you need cultural norms; you need ethical principles; you need a sense of moral behavior. This is when Gorbachev started perestroika in the broader sense as a cultural reeducation.

I also discovered on my recent trip to the Soviet Union an aspect of perestroika that is much more directly relevant to our conversation here. Gorbachev combines his political efforts, as he is leading the perestroika movement, with a language that is very close to our language. Many of the terms that we have been using throughout our conversation are terms that he uses in his speeches. In the last two years, I have been interested in exploring the roots of Gorbachev's language. How did he become familiar with this language? It's a philosophical and scientific language that he must have developed in cooperation with others. What I found out is that this "new thinking," as he calls it, has its origins in the 1970s. During that time there was a dispersed group of philosophers and scientists who explored what we would call the paradigm shift. They did so in a series of articles and roundtable discussions published in a very well known philosophical journal called *Questions of Philosophy.* The editor of that journal during the 1970s was a philosopher named Ivan Frolov, who became the editor-in-chief of *Pravda* under Gorbachev, a very close adviser to Gorbachev.

The particular slant of these explorations of new thinking in the 1970s was an exploration of the relationships between science, philosophy, religion, and art. In other words, it was more or less what we have been doing here in our dialogue. What this means to me is that the new thinking of Gorbachev is really part of one and the same movement of which we are also a part.

So conversations like the one we have been engaged in now for some time and that are presented in this book went on in the Soviet Union in the 1970s at the time when the ideas we are talking about were being worked out here, too. To put it in an extreme way, you could say that it was those kinds of conversations that ultimately brought down the Berlin Wall. Those kinds of conversations influenced the thinking of Gorbachev, who was a major influence in the political changes in Central Europe that brought down the Berlin Wall. So there is a direct link between what we have been engaged in here and the recent dramatic changes in the political landscape of Europe.

DAVID   And I can think of many invisible walls that still need to be brought down. Maybe our conversation will make some contribution to bringing them down.

Bibliography

Note: The bibliography is restricted to works mentioned in the text.

Ashvagosha. *The Awakening of Faith.* Translated by D. T. Suzuki. Chicago: Open Court, 1900.

Capra, Fritjof. *The Tao of Physics.* Boston: Shambhala, 1975; third, updated edition: 1991.

Capra, Fritjof. *The Turning Point.* New York: Simon & Schuster, 1982.

Dulles, Avery. *Models of the Church.* New York: Doubleday, 1982.

Gutierrez, Gustavo. *A Theology of Liberation.* Maryknoll, NY: Orbis Books, 1988.

Hawking, Stephen. *A Brief History of Time.* New York: Bantam, 1962.

Heisenberg, Werner. *Physics and Philosophy.* New York: Harper & Row, 1962.

Kuhn, Thomas. *The Structure of Scientific Revolutions.* Chicago: University of Chicago Press, 1962.

Lopez, Donald S., and Steven C. Rockefeller (Eds.), *Christ and the Bodhisattva.* Albany: State University of New York Press, 1987.

Maturana, Humbert R., and Francisco J. Varela. *The Tree of Knowledge.* Boston: Shambhala, 1987.

Index